Jewels
In My Journey

PEEK INTO AN ORDINARY LIFE

For information address:
J2B Publishing LLC
4251 Columbia Park Road
Pomfret, MD 20675
www.J2BLLC.com

Cover art by Brien Cole (www.briencole.com)

Printed and bound in the United States of America.

ISBN: 978-1-948747-42-4 – Paperback
          978-1-948747-43-1 – Hardcover

Jewels
In My Journey

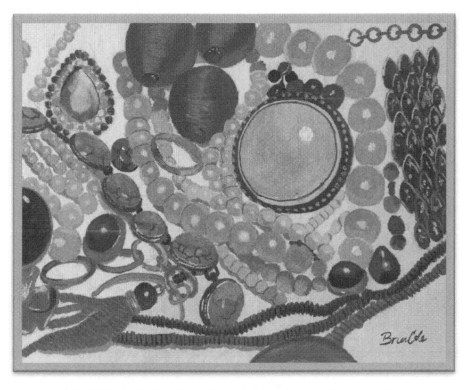

PEEK INTO AN ORDINARY LIFE

Joan Curtis Waters

 J2B PUBLISHING

ABOUT THE COVER

Orange is me. It is vibrant and bold. The color orange is most associated with amusement, activity, warmth, fire, energy, the unconventional, extroverts, taste, and aroma.

The cover art is a hand-painted rendition of several pieces in my personal jewelry collection. My eclectic collection includes something for every occasion; formal, classy chic and casual of varying hues, shapes and sizes. One ring has special significance – the gold band. It is my maternal grandmother's wedding ring; over 100 years old. The fine etching has faded over the years, but its value has not diminished. It reminds me of Grandmother Florine and Granddaddy Abraham and the family legacy they passed on to their children and children's children. Priceless!

Jewels are precious stones, signifying you and me – the women of the world. We come in all sizes, shapes and colors. We are as diverse as the jewels on the cover. The key is to celebrate and appreciate the beauty found in each of us, and ourselves. We are exquisite creations, fearfully and wonderfully made.

Jewels also represent the wisdom we acquire as we journey through life. Each jewel has a distinct level of intensity. Take time to examine lessons learned in your experiences – like examining the clarity of a diamond. Therein you will find precious jewels that prepare you for every season of life. I encourage you to be still and ask yourself what you have learned as you travel through life – insight about yourself, about your choices, about your world and people in general. Some lessons may be clearer than others. Don't despair if there is no clarity. Often, experiences have a cumulative or domino effect and it's necessary to step back and look at the whole picture to gain understanding; to truly appreciate every nugget; to fully grasp and internalize every gem of wisdom.

Lastly, a few words about the selection process for the artwork. Orange would be the central color (my fave) and I downloaded a beautiful jewels picture on the web. I realized that permission to use that graphic was required but could not find its origin. The search for another picture was fruitless. Then came the idea to use my own jewelry. I carefully selected and arranged assorted pieces; took a snapshot. Voila! - design #2. That was in April 2019. The final design came months later after engaging an exceptional fine artist to do the work. He produced the perfect design.

Sometimes we get so excited by a particular concept or desire (for things of this world) and God will whisper "I have better for you." That inner God voice speaks and seemingly out of nowhere something better comes along. And we think that's it. Then He whispers again – "This is good, but not the best for you." And we think – "what could be better than this?" Something new and even more wonderful appears on the scene; something way better than first imagined. Wait on God. Listen to His still, small voice. Hang tight and wait patiently. Don't be in such a hurry. Be still. God shows up and shows out in ways that only He can do! We might wonder why it didn't happen earlier. Too often we move too quickly, and we miss out on the better thing – the best thing. The art of being still... a valuable trait.

I encourage you to embrace your Journey.

Live to the fullest.

Share Your Unique Sparkle!

These writings are dedicated to my parents,

Bernard & Annie.

Daddy and Mama displayed solid, character-building qualities before us four children. Despite the odds, they lived loving and meaningful lives.

They were loyal, dedicated, focused,

hard-working, and fun!

Everyone witnessed their deep respect and love for each other, the Lord, and their children, extended family,

and community.

ACKNOWLEDGEMENTS

Deepest Thanks to my Cheerleaders - trusted family and friends who encouraged, assisted and prayed for this work. Their love and support kept me moving forward and extends way beyond this track of my journey. Words inadequately express how deeply grateful I am for their presence in my life. Their giving hearts bless mine to the core.

My daughters **Rashida and Jill** were the first to support and celebrate my desire to write about my life experiences. They offered wonderful insights that helped me solidify the purpose of this book and what I wanted to convey to readers. They encouraged me to write about areas of my life that I hesitated to share. While they may not want to read the "Rituals" chapter right now – I know they will appreciate it later.

My siblings, **Don and Carolyn**, have been solid prayer warriors and encouragers. I truly believe that their intercession ushered in God's inspiration. Of course, I extended to them the courtesy of reading what I wrote about them and our family before releasing this book. Do unto others! LOL.

Niece **Juanita** is a true copy editor. She noticed my strange relationship with commas, dashes, and ellipses early on. Thankfully, her keen eye found and corrected my overuse and misplacements. Quite entertaining were her attempts to make sense of my jargon and cryptic expressions. We both chuckled at phrases that made complete sense to me but apparently to no one else. She escorted me to the finish line and I REALLY appreciate that she makes me look good! I've thanked her at least a hundred times and that still isn't enough.

Gloria is a sister from another mother; aka Sister-Girl-Cousin. Gifted in her own right as a jazzy gospel artist, she has not only been an inspiration to me but, like my daughters, encouraged me to "do it!" She claims that my writing inspires her. We have ministered to women in our circle together for a number of years. It's always fun and fulfilling to work and serve others alongside her. We really don't consider it work – it's sharing our gifts and we are blessed as a result.

Deborah, my BFF and truly my Sister-from-Another-Mother, has cheered me on from the git-go. That's what we do – appreciate and celebrate each other at every turn. We met several years ago when God brought us together to serve in the women's ministry at our local church. It surely was divinely orchestrated. We've adopted each other into our respective families. So, we are sisters in both the natural and spiritual realms. I don't think she believed that I was going to do this when I first told her, because I talk about doing lots of things. Ha!

Sincere thanks to my **Bible Study sisters and brothers** for their continual prayer and excitement for this project. They know who they are. Their support continues to bless my heart more than they probably realize. I am grateful for and enjoy our friendship and being able to just be me whenever we're together.

I must give a shout-out of thanks to my new friend and fellow author, **Sera**. She graciously shared valuable tips and guidance regarding the writing and publishing process. That has been a tremendous help to this first-time author.

Although I've considered writing a book for many years, it was an unexpected encounter in the Fall of 2018 that spurred me into action. I've known **Jim & Katie,** established authors in their own right, for over 25 years and our paths cross every now and then. It's always fun catching up. I remember telling them that I had a book in me. They offered their help and invited me to a local chapter of the Maryland Writers Association where I met other authors, across a wide spectrum of literary genres. We now have something else in common – a love for writing. I am eternally grateful for their friendship and support.

I also thank **Stephanie** and **Michelle** (whom I've never met) for their objective feedback and suggestions upon review of *Jewels.* I hope that our paths will cross in the near future so that I can give them a big Thanks-Hug!

Deeply grateful is this ordinary woman for the countless family and friends who say they want a copy of *Jewels.* I've been telling lots of people about this project for one selfish reason – to keep me on track and "walking the talk" that every one of us has a story and we should share it with others. Doing so just might help someone, somewhere.

I Am Most Grateful to the Lord without whom none of this would be possible. It is a labor of love – He first loved me! How wonderful that God brings together many hands and hearts to accomplish His will. He goes before me, inspires me, guides me, loves me unconditionally, and blesses me beyond measure. I will forever praise Him!

WHAT ARE PEOPLE SAYING ABOUT Jewels?

I really enjoyed reading your Book. I liked the way you pulled the reader in to experience with you the things you experienced in your life and the relative lessons learned. You enabled your readers to become one of your family members. Anyone reading the content would be able to cry, ponder or just laugh out loud with you as you reminisced about poignant family memories or incidents in your life--and the jewels you were able to excavate out of each situation. You encouraged and engaged the reader to "create their own jewels" on their life's journey. You showed them to always look for the "hidden blessing" in any life challenge.

I, as the reader, appreciated your authenticity, candidness and courage. It takes courage to pull back the layers of one's life and share it with the world. Your literary work lets other people know "they are not alone." When you let your light shine (without fear), you automatically encourage others to do the same...

 **Sera Jordan**, Christian Teacher, Motivational Speaker and Author of Stop Existing and Live!

Your book is such a blessing and gift. I think it would be a blessing to any woman at any stage of life. I found myself especially drawn to several chapters... All the chapters had incredible nuggets of wisdom. Your honesty and openness made this book very relatable. I can see myself referring back to specific sections as I encounter various life events... I truly enjoyed it.

Stephanie, Indiana

I greatly enjoyed your book & like myself, many will find their lives within your stories. I liked the "assignments" at the end of each chapter. Readers will certainly be blessed, uplifted, encouraged, joy-filled and in search of your NEXT book, after journeying through this Jewel of a book with you. I look forward to recommending it to others!

 **Michelle,** Indiana

TABLE OF CONTENTS

INTRODUCTION

"I Have Something To Say!"

Samantha shouted these words to those around her. They were oblivious to her presence, engaged in their own conversations. It took two or three times shouting those words to get their attention, a little louder each time... She had to be louder than their noise. Finally, everyone stopped their chatter and looked her way. That's probably what she was thinking – finally! *Yes, finally, they will listen to what I have to say.*

This is actually a scene from one of my favorite comedies. It's a feel-good movie version of an old television show where love blossoms and the main characters live happily ever after. It's a fairy tale and oh, so entertaining to us romantics; a brief diversion from real life.

Some find it hard to believe that I once had an inferiority complex and was very shy. It's true. I grew up in the shadow of my siblings who I thought were so much better than me. As a young adult, I walked in the shadow of outgoing friends. No one knew I felt little. No one noticed. I guess I hid it pretty well. Didn't realize the gifts within. Maybe that's why I love movies; they are bigger than life. I would immerse myself in favorite characters.

As a single mother though, I had to step up and make things happen for my children. A boldness took over. As a self-employed jewelry consultant, I discovered that I had to sell myself to sell my products. Sales was something I vowed I would never do. (Never say never!) I developed people skills that I still enjoy today, yes *enjoy*. The secret? Take my eyes off myself and my uneasiness and focus on others – learn about them, listen. People want to feel cared for. As Maya Angelou has said:

"I've learned that people will forget what you said, people will forget what you did, but people will never forget how you made them feel."

Back to Samantha, I came to realize that I too have something to say! Wasn't there a song called "you don't have to be a star"? It's true, people like you, like me, can positively affect the lives of others if we're willing to share our truths, our experiences.

In this book, I do just that. You'll find poetic expressions, observations about life around me, ponderings, and a little humor. You will also read family tributes and memorials. This compilation of writings is a work in progress that began over eight years ago as occasional journaling. Little did I know then that one day I would be sharing them with the masses. I share because I hope to encourage and inspire women to live their best life, to appreciate all that they are, and offer it to the world.

As I considered what to share through (include in) this work, my thoughts were that giving a little peek into this ordinary life - my experiences, observations and feelings would resonate with women who feel that no one gets it, no one knows what they are going through, no one knows how they feel about this or that – the heartache, pain, disillusionment, and yearnings of their heart or the depths of their great joy. Of course, we know that many people do get it, because there is nothing new under the sun; there's no place that someone else has not been. It just seems that way when we despair or are feeling disconnected or hurt. We get so mired in our own happenings that we're unable to see the big picture and that it really is not just all about me. There's a BIGGER story.

This project is not a theological study. I'm certainly not qualified for that. My desire is to share my story in a way that connects with hearts and souls regardless of our commonalities or differences. You may not look like me or act like me, walk or talk like me, or believe what I believe, but we all share the desire to be understood, to be respected, and to be loved.

I discovered that I cannot talk about my life and learnings without mentioning my Savior Jesus Christ or talking about His undeniable presence and influence in my life. True to His word, God has never forsaken me. He has been faithful and remains "in it" with me at every turn. His love has been unwavering and unconditional. I don't want to be preachy but this is my truth, my reality. No apologies. Just fact.

I pray abundant blessings on your life and hope that you will take time to dig for the jewels within your heart; your gifts, your passions, your dreams – your greatness! May you discover the peace that surpasses all understanding.

... and the **Jewels In Your Journey.**

CHAPTER ONE

50 Shades

50 Shades of You! Have you ever taken stock of what makes you the incredible self that you are? Do you celebrate you? In this world of negativity, sometimes the good gets lost. No one really notices, or so it seems. Charity begins at home and I believe that we need to recognize the beauty within. This enables us to walk confidently – recognizing that we have God-given gifts to offer the world around us. This is not an invitation to idolize oneself but to recognize and affirm who we are.

Assignment! Take a few minutes to write down at least 50 shades of you – your top 50 attributes, gifts, and characteristics. Like me, it may take a minute and it's perfectly okay to ask those closest to you for help. They may see you differently than you see yourself. We are our own worst critics most times. A few friends shared their lists with me and that helped me complete mine. Review your list often. Update it when needed. Say them out loud. Proclaim who you are – do it for you!

This is me: Christian, African-American, divorced, mother, grandmother aka Gigi, lover of all things beautiful, a hopeful romantic, jazz lover, creative, joyful, richly blessed, classy, evolving, empathetic, sincere, fun-loving, short, bold, talkative, friendly, loving, positive, intelligent, chosen, beautiful, deserving, good enough, teachable, appreciated, successful, strong, God's masterpiece, totally feminine, gracious, devoted, anointed, growing, powerful, considerate, a winner, brave, courageous, conciliatory, gifted, caring, worthy, forgiven, silly, humble, encouraging, conscientious, prayerful, jewelry-lover, punctual, trustworthy, respectful, spontaneous, intentional, articulate, mature, faithful, whole, supportive, positive, called, visionary, optimistic, idealistic, hopeful, playful, vulnerable, trusting, affable, resourceful, unique, attentive, grateful.

CHAPTER TWO

Attitude Of Gratitude

𝔦𝔱'𝔰 𝔗𝔥𝔞𝔫𝔨𝔰𝔤𝔦𝔳𝔦𝔫𝔤 𝔪𝔬𝔯𝔫𝔦𝔫𝔤, 2018; a great time to consider all blessings received throughout the year. Once a year is not enough! Being thankful and grateful on a regular basis is paramount to good mental health. Yes, mental health. We are surrounded daily with boatloads of negativity. Reminding ourselves of what's good in this world goes a long way to maintaining a balanced perspective. What better place to start than right at home, in your conscious mind?

Do you begin/end your day with a dose of the news? How depressing is that! I got rid of cable TV for that reason – don't need to know about crimes & misdemeanors, or who divorced whom as I enjoy my morning java or relax at the end of the day. Sounds selfish, right? - To block out what's happening around me? I believe it's important to protect one's "house" and heart; to be careful about what we let in. And it makes no sense to me to release control of my thoughts to others; to allow outside forces to infect my consciousness with negative, useless, and irreverent thoughts and images. I preached to my children, "garbage in = garbage out." It's true for us all, regardless of age. I mean, how many times can the same "news" be regurgitated

3

throughout the day? Here and there you might hear a story about someone doing something good. But don't hold your breath. (I digress often.)

Attitude of gratitude, that's the subject. It may be difficult to have a grateful outlook when everything seems to be going wrong. We all have those days, weeks, months, or longer. Get this - for your own sanity in the midst of hard times, it's critical to look for "blessings in disguise" AND blessings in plain view. Believe me, I've been there, at the end of the proverbial rope many times, when it's hard to see even how to make it through the day, but somewhere in that dark cloud is always something good. It takes a little practice to have that mindset, but it's well worth it. Daily doses of gratitude, before we get to that place, makes it easier to maintain a positive outlook in difficult times.

Case in point: A dear friend of mine has a wayward daughter who once was an honor roll student. One day – and no one can pinpoint the exact day – there was a 360-degree turn in her daughter's mind and life course. It's been a little over a year since, and that beautifully gifted young person is now in the grips of drug addiction/abuse. She has made unbelievably bad choices in friends, attitude, environment, etc., and refuses help. This young lady dropped out of high school in her senior year; is dealing drugs to support her habit and harassing her parents for money. She lives with her drug-addicted, abusive boyfriend and has been jailed for shoplifting, assault and carrying a concealed weapon. She is unbelievably rude and verbally abusive towards her parents and other family members and has adopted an attitude of entitlement; they owe her. How sad! My friend and her husband have totally different approaches to all that's been happening with their daughter and that causes much tension between them. They also have other young children at home and it seems this daughter deliberately causes havoc that affects everyone.

I bring this to your attention because just today we talked, and my friend ended the "update" by stating that, while she feels totally drained and sometimes hopeless dealing with all this, she will not overlook the good things happening in her life. She named several: a job close to home and flexible so that she can attend to family matters; a strong support system (family and friends) who assist and encourage during hard times, and rejoice when victories won; strength to endure trying times; resolute faith that God has a plan for her life and everyone in her family. She made it a point to say "THANK YOU, GOD" for sustaining her and her family. She stressed that she will not let the present turmoil drown out her gratitude for the blessings she and her family, including the wayward daughter, continue to receive. Now, that's an inspiration to ME.

Years ago, as I was enduring a failing marriage and struggling to make ends meet, my faith was not diminished, even when I was laid off from one job and worked two part-time jobs during the search for another. I still trusted in God and it was important to me to stand upright and continue walking in faith, no matter how hard it was and to be thankful for the blessings I received. And there were many including: strong family support;

food on the table; a place to live; a supportive church that created a job for me as church secretary while I searched for full-time employment; good health. Our needs were met and there were special treats for my girls, courtesy of friends/family – like summer camp, sleepovers with friends, etc. Sometimes I felt like I wasn't doing enough for my daughters; I wanted them to have the world.

When I look back, it's clear to me that God was with me/us the whole time. I remember a church friend complaining to me about how bad her week was and then asked about mine. After hearing what I was dealing with, she concluded that she really had no reason to whine and complain. LOL. We then prayed for each other.

So, practice gifting yourself with doses of gratitude. Every day, write down at least five things you're thankful for. Just think how many items you'll have written down in a week or a month. Try it. Be creative. For example, throughout the day look for things that could have gone wrong but didn't. I assure you there will be a mountain of evidence of blessings. Include small and big blessings, like waking up with a sound mind; and life itself! Don't forget treasured family, friends, and a car that runs. I think you get it.

Save the lists and review them every now and then, especially when things get difficult. Being reminded that you are blessed is therapeutic and will regenerate you so you can navigate through rough waters.

The Christian faith says God's grace and mercies are limitless and every day should be Thanksgiving. I aim to appreciate every moment and show gratitude to the One who makes it all possible. And I hope that you will take time to count your blessings; that you look for them and recognize them so that you may be encouraged when life challenges come.

By the way, if you are not of the same faith - you can be. You too can receive favor in your life and begin anew. I pray God's love, peace and unconditional forgiveness for you. He wants you to have the best life, here and now. He is available 24/7. Trust Him, invite Him into your life.

 What are you grateful for? Write it down.

CHAPTER THREE

Christmas Memories

I am blessed to have happy memories of Christmas with family. These memories remind me it is worth the energy and effort to celebrate holidays and include family. I also know from personal experience that life challenges -poverty, illness, loneliness, depression- diminish the jolliness of the season and make it very hard to create good holiday memories for yourself and your children. The holiday season is not merry for everyone. To give you a vision of what is possible, I want to share my happy memories. But, before I share, I pray for those who will struggle during the holiday season, that the love of the Lord will reach them, either in the quietness of their hearts or through the kindness of others. I also pray that the Lord stirs my heart to always be grateful for my blessings and to be ready to share with others.

So, get comfy as we travel back in time. In my mind's eye, I see a Christmas tree in the living room corner - always a live tree, not store-bought. We couldn't afford store-bought and who purchases trees back then in the 50s & 60s? Daddy and the boys would brave the cold, venture into the woods behind our house, and come back with a pretty ugly tree. It wasn't a Blue Spruce,

Scotch Pine, or Leyland Cypress and we hadn't heard of a Fraser Fir. I think it was cedar and it was never perfectly shaped. To stand it upright and keep it from falling over, Daddy would tie it to the corner walls with thin string. Then lights, with the big bulbs (now popular again). Add fragile, hand-painted porcelain ornaments and homemade ones, icicles, frizzy gold or silver garland, and don't forget the "angel hair." Had to be careful with the angel hair because it could cut you. Add the star on the top, usually homemade; cardboard covered with aluminum foil. Later, we graduated to a lit star or angel. The lights reflected on the foil. It looked beautiful to us. The tree was finished when we wrapped the tree skirt around the bottom.

In our Catholic tradition, we attended Midnight Mass on Christmas Eve. That called for new outfits for my sister and me and getting our hair "papped" (meaning straightened and curled). Mama made sure her children looked their best, not just special days but every day. Sometimes, a family friend would do our hair – wash and straighten it with the dreaded hot comb. Better hold still or you'd get burned. I can feel the heat now – on my "kitchen" (hair at the nape of the neck) and the baby hair on my temples, and the hair close to my ears; had to hold down the ears to not burn them. I laughed at my sister who got burned often because she had a hard time sitting still. Miss Eva would crack open the kitchen door to let out the stench of burning hair. We loved the end product. Had to sleep on those pink sponge curlers to keep fresh curls. Love that girly thang! Oh, I digress.

Back to Christmas Eve. After church, Mama would hurry us to bed so Santa could come. According to her, he wouldn't show up if we were still up/awake. Then she'd continue cooking for Christmas and usher "Santa" in. I never saw Mommy kissing Santa Claus and can't remember if we ever actually left him a snack.

We got up around 5 or 6am to see what Santa brought. There were four of us, two boys and two girls and each would get one toy and one item of clothing. Gifts were never wrapped, but laid out on our own spot on the sofa and chairs. Can't remember my age (maybe 5) – **loved** that three-foot tall walking doll. Who cared if she was white? She became my new best friend. Besides, there were no black dolls then. Another Christmas, I got the Tressy doll with growing hair!! Loved it, then I cut her hair. Another year, a typewriter – helped me develop my superb keyboarding skills. One year, my sister and I couldn't figure out why the boys wouldn't get up with us and come downstairs to see what Santa brought. We didn't understand and just figured they were lazy. They had broken tradition. Later, they admitted that they found the gifts hidden in the attic and had already played with our toys. Boys! Ugh! But we were happy!!

Christmas morning was filled with the aroma of country sausage, homemade biscuits, fried apples... Mmmmmm. Then roasting turkey and stuffing smells would take over. It wasn't Christmas without homemade yeast rolls, mashed potatoes in a pool of gravy, Harvard beets, sweet potatoes, and kale with homemade chow-chow relish. Yum! Leftovers were great so we could have dinner for breakfast the next day... ok, all day!

Christmas dinner was always at Granny's next door with my aunts, uncles and cousins. Of course, we sat at the children's table in the kitchen while the grownups ate in the dining room. After dinner, delectable sweets emerged: homemade cakes, pies, and a variety of nuts & candies with homemade eggnog and dandelion wine, Manischewitz wine, and hard stuff I didn't know about. One year, a cousin had a mason jar with clear liquid. His eyes were red and he was grinning ear to ear. I was at the youngest end of the cousin line and he was one of the older cousins.

"What is it?" we kept asking. "White lightning" he said. We wanted to taste it, so he snuck us a sip. Whew! So strong and nasty. Ugh! I didn't like it, and have not been a fan of strong drink since. A little wine is good for me, thank you! Well, Pina Colada is tasty, too!

After dinner and dessert, the tradition was to gather everyone around the dining room table and hand out gifts. We children sat on the back stairs that led up to the bedrooms. Everyone else crowded into the dining room. Mama's siblings brought gifts for each other (usually small housewares) and all the children received small items (socks, gloves, etc.). More gifts!! We loved it.

The rest of Christmas week was progressive partying, from one house to another for desserts and games. I'll never forget being at Aunt Gina's house and Sam & Dave's "Soul Man" was playing on the record player. We all laughed and cheered on a younger cousin as he danced & pranced for us. What a fun memory!

I really encourage you to make family togetherness during holidays a priority. It will take special preparation as it seems that my generation and beyond are just too busy to stay connected. Family reunions are another step in keeping connected. As I've "preached" at our reunions – by Divine providence, we are related. We have a bond. God put us together as a family on this planet of billions of people. It's too bad that we have closer relationships with strangers from other "tribes". There's nothing wrong with having friends, but in my view, it's very wrong to put others before your own family. *Just say'n.*

Do you have joyful Christmas memories? If not, consider how you might create a few. It could be helping someone in need, or simply gathering with friends. Doesn't have to be epic, just positively memorable. And remember the true Reason for the Season!

CHAPTER FOUR

Love Letters

As I was preparing to write a love letter to a special friend, I decided that it was more important, at that point in time, to put on paper my feelings for my Father, God.

I share this with you to testify of His goodness, love and grace.

Dear Father,

I stand before You in total awe and admiration. I bow before you the Creator of all that is... the Author and Finisher of my faith. I lift my voice in worship. I write this letter as my testament that You are real.

Thank you for being ever-present – and I mean present – in my life, even when I was unaware. Not only have you given me eternal life, you are walking me through a wonderful life! And it's only just begun. You have upheld and strengthened me in every season of my life – schooling, singleness, marriage & divorce, single parenting, death of loved ones, drama and illnesses... to name a few.

You open my ears to hear your voice. Help me, Lord, to turn to you more – to hear and obey. Use me, work through me, to share your love and abundant blessings. Help me to never be too busy to do your will. Give me wisdom and discernment.

This may sound cliché, but – How do I love you? Let me recount the ways... my whys.

I love you, Lord, because You:

* ✳ *First loved me.*
* ✳ *Sacrificed your Son so that I might live.*
* ✳ *Love all your children and are no respecter of persons.*
* ✳ *Promised never to leave or forsake me, and you haven't.*
* ✳ *Have blessed me in spiritual places and are actively revealing them.*
* ✳ *Never lie. Your Word never returns void.*
* ✳ *Forgive freely and toss my sins as far as the east is from the west.*
* ✳ *Made me a new creation.*
* ✳ *Are patient and always available.*
* ✳ *Care about every area of my life – Every. Little. Thing.*
* ✳ *Gifted me with talents to enjoy and share.*
* ✳ *Gave me the ability to love, even when it's not returned.*

    ✳   *Give joy, comfort and peace that exceed my comprehension and expectations.*

Lord, there is no one like you. Your kingdom will reign forever. Every tongue will confess that you are Lord!

One more request: Give me a burning desire to truly live a life that honors You, so others might see You in me. You know the areas I need to work on. The blinders get comfy and fit too well sometimes.

From your humble servant...

Have you written a love letter lately? Choose someone special and do it. Consider dropping love notes weekly, or daily. You will bless someone and that will in turn bring joy to your heart.

CHAPTER FIVE

The Sounds Of Music

The *Sound Of Music* movie is one of my all-time favorite musicals. The title brings to mind how music has serenaded my entire life. At my retirement (aka "New Season") party, I shared with guests snippets of my life journey – in music. Notably, God has been ever-present, even when I didn't realize it.

I'm sure that many of these icons are familiar to you. It's impossible to include all the artists & songs that have serenaded me through the years – in times of joy and sadness, triumph and defeat, moments of clarity and reflection... in the quiet of my home, at the beach on a hot summer day... and in my car to break the monotony of driving – wherever and whenever.

The early years: I enjoyed the Jackson 5 (crushed on Jackie), The Supremes, Wilson Pickett, Smokey Robinson & The Miracles, Gladys Knight, Marvin Gaye, The Temptations, The Four Tops, The O'Jays, Roberta Flack, James Taylor, Tina Turner, Patti Labelle, Minnie Ripperton, Deniece Williams, and The Emotions, to name a few.

In the 70's, Disco was king! Do you remember these? – the Bee Gees, Rose Royce, KC & The Sunshine Band, and Evelyn Champagne King.

While everyone was rocking to disco, progressive jazz caught my attention... I began plugging into the sounds of Chick Corea, Ronnie Laws, Jon Luc Ponty, and Santana. My endless list of jazz favorites includes Jonathan Butler (my jazz husband), David Sanborn, Paul Taylor, George Duke, Stanley Clarke, Miles Davis, Keiko Matsui, Najee, Spyro Gyra, Warren Hill, Boney James, George Winston, Joyce Cooling, Nick Colionne, Norman Brown, and so many more. I also began to explore a little classical, Latin and world music. Of course, I still enjoyed R&B – some favorites were Aretha Franklin, Stevie Wonder, The Stylistics, Earth Wind & Fire, The Chilites, War, Chaka Kahn, and Michael Jackson.

In the late 70's, I had to change focus from myself to my new baby daughter Rashida! Nine years later, my second blessing arrived – Jill. I was now a mother and a wife!

In the 80's and 90's, musically, it was sort of a blur as I raised my daughters. They were my #1 focus. I held a variety of jobs and stayed at home for a short time after each was born. That, I would definitely not change. I worked several part-time jobs as a substitute teacher, field rep for the Census Bureau, church secretary, and owned my own business as a jewelry consultant. In the late 90s, I landed at the local electric company where I worked for 18 years and am now a retired HR professional... It was about providing for my children.

Stop!! I have to backtrack a bit... to 1979. Another milestone occurred. I met the Lord – and life as I had known it was over forever! I really became a new person. I began to see God at work in my life. My spiritual journey began and continues today.

My music choices also changed and I began listening to Gospel aka contemporary Christian music. I found it encouraging & uplifting and it helps me keep my head to the sky both in challenging times and in times of great joy. Like all the other genres mentioned, the list of Gospel artists who inspire me is long. Yolanda Adams, Tye Tribbett, Steve Green, Richard Smallwood, Mahalia Jackson, Bebe and Cece Winans, Damita, Anthony Evans, Joann Rosario, Fred Hammond, Steven Hurd, Edwin Hawkins, André Crouch, Tramaine Hawkins, Lauren Daigle and James Fortune are a few.

Several gospel songs in particular have had great impact and express what my heart truly feels. One tune talks about how God is faithful to complete the work He's begun in my life, despite obstacles... and that I must not be discouraged or give up. Another speaks what I truly believe – that the Lord is my light and salvation, so whom shall I fear? I will trust in Him and wait on Him, confident that I will see the goodness of the Lord in my life. And in another, the artist sings how I let go of all fear. I can breathe again because it's a new day; a chapter closed in my life and there's no turning back. I've decided to look forward and not behind.

In this **new season,** looking back and reflecting where I've been. I'm moving forward and I hear God saying that I don't have to worry about a thing!

That's my story! – and I'm sticking with it.

What's your story? Write it down. Revisiting may reveal hidden blessings. Like reading a book or watching a movie; sometimes we miss things the first time around.

CHAPTER SIX

Believe You Me!

It's an everyday thing. Belief.

- We believe that our vehicles will start when we turn the key.
- We eagerly believe weather forecasters and plan our days according to their advice. We prepare for storms that never materialize, just because they said so.
- We trust that airplanes will get us where we desire to go with minimal turbulence. We know not the pilot and flight attendants or whether they're qualified to do what they do.
- We trust that doctors prescribe appropriate medications and blindly take them, even after being advised of possible serious side effects, believing those little pills will make us feel better.
- We believe that restaurant chefs will not poison our food.
- We believe that our employers will pay us on time.
- We believe sticking those tiny little needles all over will cure us.

- We trust that drivers will stop at that red traffic light. We don't know them! – or their driving records or their state of mind when they get behind the wheel.
- We believe that "healthy foods" are good for us...
- We believe that the lights will come on when we flip the switch.
- We trust those who say they love us.

So, why do we not believe God? He tells us in his Word that He loves us (1 John 4:19) and will never forsake us (Hebrews 13:5). He wants us to prosper and has a plan for our lives (Jeremiah 29:11). So why do we doubt that His word is true?

Think about it: Our core beliefs may reflect our *state* of spirituality not *level* of spirituality because levels imply that one is better than the other and invites a "holier than thou" mentality. Our individual journeys are unique and personal. God is no respecter of persons and has a specific plan for each one of us.

CHAPTER SEVEN

Be Still

I've had to admit to myself that I may be a bit of a "low-level" control freak. This is a somewhat harsh reality check because my personality is to "let it flow." Life events thrusted me into the position of having to be in control, as a single mother. It morphed into auto-pilot. It was a good thing actually and caused me to stretch way beyond my comfort zone. I was responsible for the well-being of my children. My focus was providing a safe, secure and loving home. All children deserve that. I certainly had it – raised in a home where there was no arguing by my parents. They modeled deep respect and consideration for each other. My goal was to create the same - a peaceful launch pad for them to develop into caring, responsible, productive and loving adults.

Control is addictive and sometimes creeps into other areas, which is not necessarily a bad thing. But there comes a time, that one must realize and internalize the fact that we actually have little control over our lives. External events (circumstances) can change one's course in a matter of moments. Rushed decisions can have the same effect.

As a believer, I am familiar with Scripture that admonishes us to be still so we can see God at work. In my view, it's not a matter of "let go and let God." He is sovereign and it is arrogant of me to think I can "let" God do anything. He is the Creator and Sustainer of all that is.

Remembering that He is the Author and Finisher of my faith – here's the message to you, to me. I have experienced first-hand His faithfulness in many areas of my life over the years. Right now, in one very personal area, I feel Him at work in me. *Every time* I take my eyes off Him and focus on the circumstances, confusion and doubt set in. *Every time* I turn to Him about this matter, He brings clarity and peace. While I truly do not understand why things are unfolding as they are, there's no doubt in my mind that God is at work – that it is of Him and I'm in the process of a huge life-changing blessing. I feel it! I know it!!

Now, my own wisdom tries to overshadow His. And I believe it has hindered the blessing. This day, clearly God has said to me BE STILL. *Note – It is vital to have a trusted friend who shares your beliefs to remind you of His truth; who can speak His truth in a loving manner. This helps one to not be swayed by erroneous thoughts and endless questioning.

I confess that being still at this juncture is very difficult for me because I want to help things along… you know, make sure the blessing comes to fruition. I want it now; to see it developing on a daily basis. I know better and it's a moment-by-moment challenge. Having said that, I know in my heart that He knows best and that His timing is perfect and I rest in Him. I pray for the patience that He lavishes on me. It is a work in progress.

Practice being still. Listen to that still voice; the voice of God. That may require turning off the noise (TV, radio, cell phones, PC, etc.).

CHAPTER EIGHT

Clutter

Who brought all this stuff into my house? Never been a white glove person but clean feels good. Housecleaning is a necessary evil. By no means am I a hoarder. Stuff just multiplies by itself it seems. Maybe I need a chronic clean gene, although quite content without it. There's a name for that, right? I'd much rather be away from home so I'm not constantly reminded of those beloved household chores; like at the beach, or the movies; distracted from reality.

No surprise visits, please. Call before you drop by! Truthfully, you don't need to see my mess. I trust that you will not share that everything's just tucked behind closed doors.

Deeper meaning? Of course, but let's not go there right now. Well, just a few words. We all hide a lot of our stuff. We want people to see everything bright and shiny – absolutely not what we tuck under the bed and in the closet; the messy parts of our lives. You know your "issues." **Everyone has issues**.

Too often, we are only fooling ourselves by trying to ignore the elephant in the room. Acting as if we don't see the obvious, we choose to not face the truth in our own minds. We justify and sometimes ignore reality and say *"Whatever!"* - choosing not to deal with areas that truly need attention and action.

Have you ever just dug in to resolve or improve an issue? It's actually a great feeling to get resolution and closure. The digging may not be fun but the result typically brings peace. Please do resist the temptation of self-condemnation. That would be self-defeating. Just keep moving forward and when tempted to put the blinders back on, tackle it head-on. Just do it! I'm talking to myself here.

Maybe you can relate. Have you tended to your secret areas? It's necessary to grow. If ignored, little things often become big things.

CHAPTER NINE

Cloud Of Witnesses

While visiting with my niece in Indianapolis, she pointed out her display of funeral programs for beloved family members who have passed on from this life. Hold on, it's a positive thing. She keeps them in plain view as reminders and refers to them as her *Cloud Of Witnesses*. That phrase has biblical origin. The book of Hebrews in the New Testament talks about believers of old who are examples of strong faith. They looked forward to the coming of the Messiah. They believed God and lived their lives by faith.

My niece proudly looks to the forefathers (and mothers) in our family as examples of strong men and women who paved the way for us. On their shoulders we stand. They worked hard, provided for their families, unhesitatingly shared the love and taught us valuable life lessons as they lived their own.

I am proud to join her in honoring my immediate *Cloud Of Witnesses* – my parents, my youngest brother and my parents-in-law. I do so because they helped make me the woman I am today. Their wisdom, support and guidance at particular junctures of my journey are invaluable. They are lovingly remembered.

60 Days

FOR MY MOTHER
Written August 2011

I'm not really counting the days since she departed this life. It just comes to mind automatically... tears come... unexpectedly... at any time... any place... I hear her voice... I still have the last phone message she left. She was just checking on me. That's what we did regularly... check on each other. I have to think of something funny right now, or the tears will come again.

It dawned on me one Sunday evening... when I felt totally alone. It was a strange feeling for me. I've never been one to "feel lonely" because I am content with or without people around me... and I always had her. Not used to feeling needy but that's how I felt. Most Sundays I would be at her house and this particular Sunday, a few weeks after her departure... I really felt alone. And I realized something.

Mama – Mrs. Annie! – would at times wonder aloud why the Lord was keeping her here, in this life... in the state she was in... in her mind unable to be of help to anyone. She disliked that she required a high level of care. She was used to being the caregiver and she was uneasy and uncomfortable being on the receiving end. Here's the thing – in her bedridden state (five years in all), she was a blessing to everyone who visited or did

32

anything for her. Yes, there were unpleasant and physically painful times. Yet, when you spent time with her, guess who left laughing and smiling? Everyone! Many told us that they enjoyed being with her even when she was not able to get around.

So, I said to her that maybe it wasn't about her; that the Lord kept her here so long so that we could be the sons and daughters that we should be caring for her as she had done for us as we grew into adults.

I don't think she really believed it! But I know it's true. The fact is, <u>we</u> needed <u>her</u>. I needed her more than she knew; more than I realized myself. I needed to know that no matter what the "world" dealt me – she was there for me. And without fail, she was. She was God's tangible love for me. I knew it in my heart, but until that moment had never realized the true depth of it.

I miss you, Mama. Every. Day. Love you more and more. Every. Day. Words can't express the impact you made on my life. Remember that day I said all this to you? We cried and laughed about this and that. And I told you not to worry about your baby girl. God would continue to watch over me when you were gone. He has. He is. Can't wait to see you in Glory!

No Middle Name

FOR MY FATHER

I was blessed with the best parents ever! My father had a third-grade education and that did not stop him from providing for his family. For many years, he did seasonal work on the road crew. Say "Thank You" when you travel along Route 5 in Southern Maryland! He was an outdoors kind of man; worked on his family farm as a youngster, which accounts for his not completing school. Later in life, he landed a job with the National Park Service as a landscape technician. He loved it and tended to our "estate" as well. He enjoyed crabbing, fished occasionally, and shucked oysters for a local crab house. He was a no-frills homebody who loved a good card game, especially with his brothers. A quiet man, he was a devoted family man. I also remember him saying at the dinner table: "There's a time to talk and a time to eat; now's the time to eat!!" He developed an aversion to different foods touching on his plate and was thoroughly unhappy whenever Mama would load his plate with food. If looks could kill! Yes, a man of few words - until playing cards with his brothers!

Daddy had an identical twin brother... thus **no middle name.** Not sure why. Maybe his Mama was so tired that she said forget extra names?!! Anyhoo, Daddy and his twin got a kick out of fooling us chillen and the grandchillen, pretending to be each other. The only way you could tell them apart was how they shaved their moustaches. We fell prey to their tricks every time! I don't know why we never caught on.

When we were youngsters, on any given Saturday, he would take my sister and me to a local park to play. Sometimes a couple cousins would join us. By the way, this park was purely a stretch of grassy area between the highways near home. This was before playgrounds with swings & slides. There were just a couple of picnic tables but we thought it was a treat to spend time there watching the cars pass. Didn't take much to entertain us back then!

Daddy was 49 when I was born. He drove the slowest Chevy on the planet. Maybe it wasn't the car! Crossing an intersection meant waiting for every vehicle in sight to pass. He was in no rush, ever! He was also known in our family circle to bed down at 8pm no matter what was going on around him, simply because he had to rise early for work. When we had company over, he would politely thank everyone for coming, invite them to stay as long as they liked and then excused himself. No joke. We chuckle about that to this day.

An uncomplicated man... I think having no middle name suited him. One might think that this modest and humble man could not positively impact anyone's life. Not so! My daddy was not a doctor or lawyer; did not even possess a high school diploma. Nothing fancy. He was a life instructor who led by example. He showed us what loyalty to family and friends looked like. His work ethic was beyond compare. His giving and genuine heart was quite evident. He just put his nose to the grindstone and did what was necessary for his family. He attended church every Sunday and prayed with us nightly. Never disrespected my mother or lifted a hand. He didn't have to yell to get his point across. Now, that was a real-life lesson for a healthy marriage. I had culture shock when I left the nest. Literally! I learned quickly that the world can be very cruel, impersonal and inconsiderate.

Although a homebody, Daddy and Mama did socialize and had a tight-knit circle of friends. Most were family members. They enjoyed date nights, attending local dances and gatherings, although I don't remember ever seeing him cut a rug. He did a little travel with Mama but preferred being at home. His favorite snack was her homemade spice cookies. He had no idea that they were carrot cookies. He didn't like carrots. I jokingly teased my mother that I was going to spill the beans, but we never told him.

What I miss most is that quiet spirit and any opportunity to sit and chat… to really get to know the man, my father, on a personal level.

Thanks, Daddy for taking time for us. We remain close to our cousins, thanks to you. Miss you lots and love you forever!

Irk, Bubs, GMC

LETTER TO MY BROTHER

Well, dear Brother, I think it's time to put on paper what I really think of you... My heart is full as I think of all the fun we had over the years. There were very few times we disagreed on anything. I forgive you for scaring me in the dark when I was your trusting little sister. I forgive you for eating the food off my plate and finishing off my ice cream cone because you ate yours fast. Remember, we would see who could make theirs last the longest. When I did, you'd eat it! I forgive you for only giving me and Sissy a quarter for cleaning your stinking room back in the day or was it just a nickel? You cheapskate! I forgive you for bowing out as we were planning a surprise 60th birthday party for you, as if you had any control over that. There must be something else I need to forgive you for!

In case you didn't hear me as we stood at your bedside during your final hours, thank you for everything you did for me and the girls when times were hard. You know I appreciate that. Thank you for being you – a loving and dedicated son, brother, husband and father. A real giver! I'll never forget the stories that your in-laws shared when we gathered at your house – not that I didn't already know. Nope, you weren't there. Or maybe you were. It made me so proud to hear again about your unselfish giving when anyone needed a little help - much less your church family! I am forever proud to call you brother. Miss you way too much! (smile) and love you forever. By the way, I heard you say in my ear that you got me into Arlington National Cemetery. That was not necessary. Can't wait to see you again.

Your FAVORITE sister...

China Closet

FOR MY MOTHER-IN-LAW (2011)

There they sit… fragile, pristine, awaiting a new holiday… beautiful gold etching along the border, hand-painted floral design; carefully stacked, protected, behind the glass doors. Seen but rarely used and only for special people on special days. That was my perception of the dainty ware, only released in their glory during traditional holiday seasons.

But that changed. My perception changed when I met her. She is lovely, loving, caring, adorable, funny, and engaging. Miss Claire is my other Mom and she taught me an important life lesson that day. I first met her over 40 years ago and she made an indelible impression.

On an ordinary day she served her family, routinely, with china that was meant to be enjoyed, not stored away for the "special" people, visitors, the company who came to celebrate a holiday. Miss Claire, my other mother, taught me how important a small gesture can be. She believed that her family was of ultimate importance, her heart, and deserving of that fine china on any day.

We celebrated her 100th birthday this year with fine china - on the lawn, in the backyard. The special people, her family, came from near and far that particular day. It was so appropriate to honor her with this small gesture; returning the love she freely gives.

I see her smile, hear her laughter and her secret whispers. She is a gem and I was blessed to be in her inner circle who enjoyed breaking bread with her; whether ordinary fare or delicacies.

She is beautiful, in and out... delicate and fragile. *OraLee, I'll never forget Assateague in December – freezing cold! And sitting on the front porch and the OC boardwalk. I miss you and love you dearly!!*

Tribute To Pop-Pop

FOR MY FATHER-IN-LAW (2011)

God took the strength of a mountain,
The majesty of a tree,
The warmth of a summer sun,
The calm of a quiet sea.

The generous soul of nature,
The comforting arm of night,
The wisdom of the ages,
The power of the eagle's flight.

The joy of a morning in spring,
The faith of a mustard seed,
The patience of eternity,
The depth of a family need.

Then God combined these qualities,
When there was nothing more to add,
He knew His masterpiece was complete,
And so, He called it ... Dad
(anonymous)

Dad, I can hear your melodic voice and hear your laughter.
Back in the day, Anthony's surely had the best roast beef

sandwich in OC! – your favorite. Miss you and will forever love you madly! (wink)

As you might imagine, I have a lifetime of great memories with these special people. They played significant roles in my life, individually and together. We enjoyed each other and did a lot of laughing! My children are my in-laws' only grandchildren and that earned me a special place in their hearts. I made every effort to engage them in my children's lives and they appreciated that to no end.

Being the youngest child, I also held a special place in my immediate family. Actually, I was a surprise addition to the family – the last one to arrive. And, according to the doctors, should be a vegetable today. One of my lungs collapsed at birth and I was given a 50/50 chance of survival; and predicted to be a vegetable if survived. I'm a miracle baby!

Who would you include in your *Cloud Of Witnesses*? They may not be blood-relatives.

CHAPTER TEN

Bittersweet Writings

2010: As My Oldest Daughter's Wedding Approached

Oh Lord, I pray for a restful night as we enter
the last few days of my daughter's singlehood.

No matter what, her happiness is paramount and I'm surprised at my own emotions as I will soon "give her away"... not really away, but away. This is the final push out of the nest; the true cutting of the umbilical cord. She will soon be joined to another to make their nest; the continuous circle of life.

My firstborn. Been keeping a lot of feelings to myself because I truly celebrate her wonderful life; the firstborn of someone who was not expected to live at birth. It's not about me. But I have to look back to be able to look forward - to truly appreciate the journey, her journey.

A brilliant child grown into a brilliant woman - a caring and kind person, motivated to immerse herself in the trenches to provide educational opportunities for kids from impoverished homes. I admire her tenacity, resolve, intelligence; so many things. She is humble, never seeking attention or wanting to be in the spotlight.

Truly a blessing to be her Mom. God has been faithful thru the years providing our needs and the desire to live upright before Him. It's still a process.

I love her so much and appreciate the relationship we now have; one that neither of us thought possible. Our honest and open love for each other is deep and profound. We agree to disagree, sort of. She has brought so much joy to my heart in ways she'll only understand as her baby boy grows. She feels it already. There's nothing on earth as special and life-changing as being a mom.

The Push Is On

The wedding train is preparing to pull out. Check the packing list to be sure nothing is forgotten: dress, shoes, jewelry, makeup, camera, etc., etc. No more tears. Ok, many tears of joy to come. Three days from this moment, we will be applying finishing touches to the bride before she becomes the Mrs. Pics and more pics. Yes, a bit nervous we'll be. My mind's eye will see her reading a newspaper upside down at the tender age of six months. LOL, so cute, my baby! First day of school, kindergarten graduation, majorette marching & trophies, piano recitals, pom squad. Fast forward to high school and college graduations, then Harlem, NY to teach. So many great memories and my heart is ready for more, new memories to cherish.

I have to stop and bow before Him who made a way when my eyes saw none. So grateful for His love! For the gift of motherhood and family and cherished friends near & far. Back to packing!

It's sweet to remember special times… and share. You never know how your story might relate to and bless someone else.

CHAPTER ELEVEN

April Fools

Isn't April Fool's Day fun? It takes creative thought to carry out "gotcha!" moments for family and friends... and friendly enemies? Oh, who said that?!

I'll never forget how I played my coworkers a few years ago. The office building was three stories with an open lobby and stairwell. Pretty nice. I strategically planted phone messages for staff from "people" like Mr. Ali Gator, Mrs. Lyon, Miss Kitty. You get the idea. All the phone numbers were the same – to the National Zoo. I waited about ten minutes and like clockwork, they all came out of their offices at the same time looking for me. It was like a movie, with me standing at a point where I could see them all. Can still see it in my mind's eye. They had the message slips in their hands and looked puzzled because they called the phone number and got the zoo's recorded message. Of course, they thought maybe I transposed the numbers. When they saw each other, the light went off and it seemed like they called my name in unison. It was hilarious! We all laughed. The Director shook her head and remarked that someone apparently didn't have enough work to do (looking at me). With a big smile I said that it's good to laugh every now and then. She shook her head again and agreed. Then we all went back to business as usual.

There's another April Fool's Day that is etched in my mind. It was 2008, the day my divorce was finalized. Yup, my divorce was officially granted and signed on April Fool's Day. When I opened the envelope and read the effective date, I hollered and fell out laughing. Now, that's hilarious! But no joke. What is most memorable is the actual feeling of a weight lifting off my shoulders. I didn't expect that. I remember it clearly. Wow, I'm free! It was a significant moment because I had been separated for many years and finally came to the point where I said enough! It's time to get on with my life, to move forward. And that I did.

During my separation, I never dated. Had no desire to date. You might think, "Sure Joan." It's true - the 'party girl' had no desire to strike up new friendships especially with the opposite sex. That's supernatural!

Disclaimer: Contrary to popular belief (LOL), I don't desire to be the center of attraction at every function. I truly had to overcome shyness – afraid of what people might think of me; wanting to make a good impression as a respectable person. I wanted to be noticed but deep down I felt that I represented my family and never wanted to indulge in anything anywhere that would cause me to be out of control. Even as a young club-hopper (that was my world as a young adult), I did not want to be remembered as the wild thang, if you get my drift. But I always enjoyed a fun party, and still do. I really love bringing folks together for a great time. I'm reminded of my Mama who said she liked seeing lots of cars in her driveway; family and friends gathered to enjoy time together. We're so much alike... but it doesn't have to be at my house! (smile)

Back to the subtopic: Though separated, I was still legally married. My #1 focus was my two daughters. But now MY TIME was about to begin. Interesting isn't it, how life comes full circle. I was already living alone so that wasn't new. What was new was that I was again free to expand my horizons! It was like a flashback to younger years.

At that point in 2008, I decided to get reacquainted with Joan. I had been in Mommy mode for a long time and absolutely loved it! I did a lot of soul searching and the single Joan began to emerge. It's funny. My daughters remarked several times: "Who *are* you?" They had only seen the Mommy side of me. I then became intently interested in my own personal development. I wanted to be the best me and was feeling that I had lots of work to do. This may not have been evident to others because I've always been the positive, happy person. And I truly am a happy person.

But I wasn't satisfied. I wanted to work on me. I began reading more and listening to great speakers like Les Brown, John Maxwell, Willie Jolley, Zig Ziglar, Tony Robbins and Jim Rohn. These were top choices because their messages were not only motivational but truly inspiring. This was the time I learned the importance of positive affirmations. There are many more authors and speakers with similar messages. Some may be addressing business-related topics yet the principles shared easily relate to one's personal life.

Right now, I'm reading a very interesting book about self-talk. Can't move on to chapter four yet because the first three chapters are so rich and deep. First thing I learned about was neuroplasticity which means that the brain can adapt and change, and it happens the fastest with repetition. We can rewire our brains! Scientifically proven. Does this not relate to the power of the tongue? If I say something over and over and over, the brain adapts to that belief. I strongly encourage you to read about positive thinking and self-talk. And instead of watching fake news and trash TV, invest in yourself by reading more.

That April Fool's Day ushered me into a new season and I was ready, sort of. It's been an awesome journey! Believe me, like everyone, I've had really hard times but more importantly I've had blessings beyond my imagination. This writing exercise is part of that and I look forward to a bright future. I like to say I'm living my BLESSED best life! It's a fabulous place to be. I embrace it totally and am not fearful of any challenges down the road. I know there will be times in the valley, as well as on the mountaintop. God is good!

Life transitions provide times for reflection and growth, and may not be most pleasant... It gets our attention. Maybe it's a call to action, to change course, a time to be still or just to take notice of where one is. There's always something to learn (or relearn) and a reason for everything. Keep your head to the sky!

CHAPTER TWELVE

It's A Wonderful Life

𝕵𝖆𝖛𝖊 𝖞𝖔𝖚 𝖘𝖊𝖊𝖓 this classic movie released in 1947? It tops my list of favorite movies. The legendary actors Jimmy Stewart and Donna Reed play the lead roles. It has been colorized but that was totally unnecessary in my view. My Christmas Eve tradition has been watching this movie as I wrap gifts, with a little eggnog on the side.

Why is the movie my best-liked? The message. It's all about the message. The movie demonstrates how one life affects many – with a little romance, humor and drama woven throughout. It's a feel-good movie. My kind of movie!

Without giving away the entire storyline... The main character is an ordinary man who becomes desperately frustrated when circumstances drive him to thoughts of suicide. On Christmas Eve, a bumbling angel, trying to earn his wings, saves him. The man expresses that he's worth more dead than alive. The angel grants his wish of never being born. They travel back in time witnessing just how different life would have been without his presence. The world he knew was very different because he wasn't in it. He soon realized the good he could bring to others, including his own family. It is a must-see movie about the gift of life.

Again, I love the message in the movie and think great lessons lie within. What do you think of your life? Do you think you impact the lives of others? The answer is a resounding "Yes!" We all have opportunity to bring joy *or drama* to the lives of those in our circles. That's a choice that we make daily, whether conscious or subconscious. Will we be self-centered or truly care for others? Do we invite others to our pity parties? It's so true that misery loves company. Goodness, how does that outlook/demeanor affect others? Will we choose to put the needs of others before our own or just get what we can for ourselves? Are we a blessing or a hindrance?

I desire to pour into others as much as I can and that brings great joy to my heart. I certainly am the recipient of much love, help and support through the years. No woman is an island. How and what that looks like may be different for each of us. It can be as simple as sharing a smile or running an errand or lending an ear when someone just needs a friend. It's really not difficult to do and when we do so, we actually receive blessings as well. It's a good feeling to know we've helped someone, especially while expecting nothing in return. Everyone needs help some time. No one is exempt from life's troubles. In my view, bringing smiles and being a help to someone, no matter how small or seemingly insignificant, is truly what makes life wonderful.

Do you have a favorite movie? What makes it a fave? Most movies have a common theme – good vs evil. Notice what happens in your favorite flick – good message, or not so much? Don't forget your favorite music; what messages do you hear?

CHAPTER THIRTEEN

Rituals

Two funerals in two weeks. Extended family members. One memorial service was Protestant, the other Catholic. Both were pretty standard. Celebrations of Life – that's what we call it now. But many don't really seem truly celebratory. It is customary to greet the family, view the body, read the obituary, sing favorite hymns, hear remembrances from family and friends, give the eulogy, then burial, ending with the repast. Somber. Ceremonial. Mentally exhausting and draining. It is tradition, accepted as part of the grieving process, and it surely is a final farewell from devoted and loving family and friends.

Thinking too of baby dedications and baptisms; different but the same in that they also are ceremonial. It is proper to be orderly on these occasions. I will never forget the memorial service for a close friend who passed away a few years ago. She planned it herself, knowing that her earthly presence was coming to a close. She selected the music, speakers, everything. Rather than the traditional religious music, she had her favorite jazz and R&B music serenade friends and family as we gathered to memorialize her. Pretty cool, in my opinion. It was a genuine reflection of her. The service ended with a video about gratefulness. Surely there wasn't a dry eye in the room and it was the most moving and impactful service I've ever attended. I'm sure that was her plan; so that we would never forget what was dear to her heart and important in this life. She lived in full color!

Celebrate Life! So, I'm stealing from her. She would say, "You go, Girlfriend!" This is what I want my life memorial to be like. Yes, I will communicate my wishes to my children (they don't want to think about it yet, they said). It will be my last Orange Party! I wish to be cremated so that money normally spent on caskets and burial (what a racket that is) can be used for a beach vacay for my family. No viewing of my dead body. No comments like – Oh, she looks so alive! Actually, I will still be alive – the real Joan, my spirit, will never die. Just like yours.

Here's the tentative plan. If they change it, I'll never know, right? And you know I'm a planner at heart!

All-Orange Celebration of Remembrance Honoring Joan Curtis Waters

- ➤ Program begins with a comedian or strolling magician.
- ➤ Live Jazz band or a Flutist... scratch that. Save money and pipe in my fave tunes.
- ➤ Photo display; no flowers. Donation box for a favorite charity, yet undecided.
- ➤ Roast & Toast by family & friends. There will be a basket of suggested toasts, in case folks can't think of anything to say because they're overtaken with grief

(LOL). Would love everyone to share/hear the funniest times we had together.

➢ "Life Is For the Living" or the "I See Dead People" talk. You'll have to be there to get the message.

➢ Laugh Therapy session right after the Eulogy (I'm practicing right now).

➢ Orange Punch (sugar-free, please) with Homemade Pound Cake & Cheesecake Bites. Something wet and something dry – perfect & simple combination for any party. My immediate family and most intimate circle of friends will have a private catered dinner or dinner at my favorite restaurant. They know the place.

➢ Keepsake – Bright orange refrigerator magnet with the words "Pay It Forward."

How would you like to be remembered? You just might be among someone's *Cloud of Witnesses*! See Chapter Nine.

CHAPTER FOURTEEN

Picture This

Yes, I like to have fun. You might enjoy this story, ripped from the pages of my own life on the job. I laugh out loud whenever I think of it.

It was a quiet afternoon at work just before a holiday weekend. I was the only person in the office. My good friend and coworker had beautiful artwork in her office space that depicted a tropical beach scene. We sat at opposite ends of the office. Several times I threatened to take her painting and hang it behind my desk. On this particular day, I decided to switch my artwork for hers, just to see if she would notice. I gingerly removed both pictures and hung mine in her area first. Then I hung her artwork behind my desk, took a few steps backward to admire it and make sure it was hanging straight. Then...

Crash! It fell to the floor and the glass shattered into a million pieces. I can still see it in my mind's eye. It was very loud and I expected someone to come running from the adjoining office to see what happened. Nothing. No one came and I just stood there in disbelief. Ugh! How was I going to explain this?! Immediately I found the facilities man to help clean up the mess. And he did, laughing the whole time. I laughed too, nervously trying to get my story together. I sweated the whole weekend. If my memory serves me correctly, after cleanup I quickly brought my artwork back to my desk and hung it in its original spot. Beautiful!

Monday morning comes. When I arrived, several others were already there and I could hear my supervisor talking loudly about the missing artwork. Uh-Oh! I knew I had to come clean. As I approached my supervisor, he was still asking around if anyone knew about the missing pic. Of all times for him to go to her office; a little unusual but it was what it was. My coworker had not arrived yet.

Here goes, I thought! I explained to my supervisor what happened the Friday before and secretly hoped that I would not be required to pay out of pocket for a replacement. Thankfully, he thought it was hilarious! Whew! A bit embarrassed, I stressed that it was a joke gone bad. He really did think it was funny and told me not to worry about it. My coworker didn't see the humor and said she would get me back. You know, payback is a ____! I thought it wise to tone down my tricks at the office after the incident and I did for a while. So glad my supervisor had a sense of humor! Ha, I can still hear the glass shattering!

What's the craziest thing you've ever done? Enjoy life, loosen up, smell the roses!

CHAPTER FIFTEEN

You Gotta Laugh!

I love to laugh. I bet you've laughed til it hurts and you can't sit or stand up straight. It doesn't take much for me, really. I can find humor in just about anything... like my siblings. My brothers and I have a special bond in humor. Some don't quite get it. Those who know us have witnessed our hilarity. I wasn't gonna go here, but I'm here now.

For instance, we gave my oldest brother a surprise 60th birthday party (and he IS older than dirt). It was like someone turned on the spotlight and we performed as never before. We confessed a few childhood antics that Mama never knew... (Ok, I told on them. I spoke of the time the boys snuck out of the house and pushed the car down the driveway to the road so our parents wouldn't hear them start it. It was time that Mama knew what they did!) LOL. We gave Oscar-worthy performances that night. Many guests remarked that we should take our "show" on the road! It was no show. It was real life. We actually loved it more than anyone else. Mama just shook her head. Priceless! Wish we had recorded it. It lives on in our memories. I could fill a book with our capers. The beauty of it is that it's all in jest. We really don't take it seriously. We just carry on and laugh with (and at) each other and enjoy every silly moment. If you saw my siblings, you'd know why! (That's a joke.)

I can't resist sharing a little more. My older-than-dirt brother called me several years ago, right after New Year's, to announce that his resolution was to stopping kidding me. Of course, I let him know that I did not make that resolution, so be prepared for the usual. Now, I've been subjected to ongoing ribbing – no, torture – by him and our brother, now deceased. He's still here, by the way. I hear his laughter as I write this, and visualize him grinning and twirling a toothpick in his mouth. So, the two of them took pleasure in scaring my sister and me in the dark when we were kids, or throwing our homemade biscuits across the dinner table. Ha, their punishment was never as severe as I thought it should be. And their story is that they dropped me on my head as a baby – which explains why I am the way I am today (their words).

Ok, so my old brother made this resolution and I interpreted that as I could turn up the heat; which I did, egging him on at every opportunity. He was tempted on many occasions to throw a friendly insult but resisted for about a year. I tried my best to get him to cave in by insulting him in a loving way. LOLOLOL! I can still see his facial expressions, trying to hold back. I want you to know that he broke that resolution. No time or space here to explain the details. Of course, he denies it and it's no surprise that his buddies take his side. Cowards!

My one and only sister, and self-proclaimed second mother, used to get pretty irritated by all the joking and told us to stop it. We looked at each and said "NOT gonna happen!" She has since come around and joins in. One day she will acquire the level of expertise that we already enjoy. Maybe.

This is the crème-de-la-crème: I am the youngest and no doubt the favorite. But definitely not spoiled. Mrs. Annie, the disciplinarian extraordinaire, didn't believe in spoiling her children to that brat status. And, contrary to popular belief, I did not always get my way because I'm the youngest. None of that! I got the same spankings as the others. And you know that I was totally innocent except that time I cut the bathroom towels with a pair of scissors. Mama tricked me into a "false" confession. LOL. I digress.

My mother and I had a special bond because our personalities were so much alike. And there's a reason I was her favorite. So, Mama shared a secret and made me promise not to tell the others while she was alive. A few months after she passed, I invited my "siblings" over because I had something important to tell them. They came over, not sure if I told them they needed to sit for the news, but I shared the secret; and that is that I am my parents' ONLY natural-born child. And they were actually adopted. No joke! I had no idea because those hoodlums were already on the scene when I arrived. Maybe that's why my brothers dropped me on my head.

They didn't believe my story for one second. You can imagine their reaction, and it has not changed. One brother commented: "You made me drive an hour to hear this nonsense?!" Understandably, they are having a hard time accepting the real truth and are in denial. It is a harsh reality! I totally understand how they must feel. If there's any physical resemblance, it's because we spent so much time together. You know how it's said that you start to look and sound like people you are around a lot. That's what happened here. But the truth is that I am an only child! This demonstrates the admirable character of my parents – loving, accepting, giving, considerate. They had pity on those three and took them in. Isn't that so touching? Let me grab a tissue. If you're ever around my siblings and the topic comes up, please be sympathetic and kind. They may never be able to truly accept the truth. I recommend counseling!

I think this is the best "gotcha!" prank I've ever pulled on my siblings. Don't tell them that I told you about it. You know that if I put in print that they really are my blood siblings, the joke is over. So, keep it to yourselves, please. What I'm about to say is the real truth – they weren't adopted. My brothers won't be reading this and I trust you not to tell! My sister read the draft so she won't see this either. Hee-hee! I know my secret confession is safe with you, right? If they come to me, I'll know you told. Don't let me down.

You GOTTA laugh! It's a proven fact that laughter is good for the body, mind and soul. Once upon a time, I kept a joke jar on my desk at work. Doing so was a suggested assignment from a webinar about handling stress. Yes, my colleagues were delighted that I insisted they grab a joke from the jar. Not! I know in my heart they appreciated the gesture to bring a smile. Here's a sample of the type of jokes I shared. Just laugh!

1. What has one head, one foot and four legs?
2. Did you hear the joke about the roof?
3. David's father has three sons: snap, crackle and _____?
4. What do you call cheese that's not yours?
5. What kind of coffee was served on the Titanic?
6. What do you call a boomerang that doesn't work?
7. What type of music are balloons scared of?

(answers on next page)

Answers:

1. A bed
2. Never mind, it's over your head!
3. David
4. Nacho cheese
5. Sanka
6. A stick
7. Pop music

What makes you laugh? Always be ready to share a little joy. A genuine smile will do.

CHAPTER SIXTEEN

Black Coffee

I was addicted to sugar for many years, actually most of my life. Sweet drinks were the norm; was raised on sweet Kool-Aid, lemonade and, of course, sweet tea. *Sweeeet* tea, Aaah! With lots of "tingle" as my Aunt Gina called it. Lots of ice. Yum! Add freshly baked homemade yeast rolls, and I'm in heaven. Comedian Flip Wilson said "The last sip of iced tea should be as sweet as the first." Yessiree! Not bragging (too much), but I made the best sweet tea. My family said I should bottle and sell it. There is a secret. Don't tell anyone! You add the sugar to the hot, freshly brewed tea, then dilute and add ice. Promise me you'll keep the secret.

Also, at the top of my sweet drinks list was Pepsi. I belonged to the NOW generation. I drank it like water; everywhere, anytime. Many nights ended with Pepsi. It was my caffeine fix. No wonder I couldn't sleep!

A few years ago, I was grossly overweight and not at all happy with my appearance or how I felt physically. I began a weight loss regimen and realized the #1 thing I had to face was my addiction to sugar. I started paying attention to what I consumed and cut out the sugar.

Coffee! What about the coffee? I adjusted pretty well to no sugar; to no sodas or sweet drinks, except coffee. It wasn't as hard as I imagined it would be. Just had to change my mind, my way of thinking because consuming sugar was killing me. But I rebelled when it came to coffee. Can't I just have one sweet drink? I said yes to that, including sweet creamers. Dark roast coffee was my preference with lots of sugar and creamer. A friend once said she likes her men and her coffee the same – light & sweet! Sounded good to me at the time. LOL. But I digress.

I soon realized that the sweet coffee had to go. So, I switched to natural sweeteners but still sometimes added sweetened creamers. That's sugar!

Long story short, or not so short: I decided to try black coffee. No sweetener of any kind and no creamer. (Yes, Joan, that is the definition of black coffee.) Surprisingly, I liked it. I could actually taste the coffee. Through the years, I had said I'd never drink black coffee. Well, never say never. My palate will adjust, I told myself... and it has. I won't say that's my preference. Now I enjoy bulletproof coffee. That's another story for another time. Right now, I think I'll make a cup of java.

Until next time, this is Miss Annie's Baby Girl signing off.

Have you had to give up something because it's not good for you? This just might be a nudge to do it now. *Just say'n!*

CHAPTER SEVENTEEN

Online Dating

So, I debated whether or not to talk about this... considered writing a book for middle-aged women on the dating scene. But can I just vent for a minute? Not into male-bashing; just sharing a few experiences and observations.

Online dating is something that I vowed I would never do, and it is not for the faint of heart! (LOL - This is the third thing I said I'd never do but did. Do you see a pattern here?) My daughters encouraged me to go this route because they wanted me to have someone special in my life. My world really had been them, church, work and gatherings with family and close friends only. I was not interested in dating. Even though separated for many years, I was still legally married. My focus was my children. After my divorce on none other than April Fool's Day ten years ago... Go ahead and laugh. I do every time I think about it and wonder if there's a hidden message in there somewhere. Seriously, I really think it's hilarious! (See Chapter 11).

So, I sign up on a popular site for African Americans – 'cause that's who I am. (Ha!) Craft a thoughtful profile description of myself and what I desire in a relationship. Ok, it is a bit long but I like to write and I want to weed out anyone who isn't like-minded spiritually. Pick a nice screen name. Post a few pics after a photo shoot at my daughter's place. Plain and simple. Turn off the computer.

A few days later, I log into the website and my inbox is jammed with flirts and messages from interested guys. Wow, a bit overwhelming to say the least! So, I get busy combing through the messages and intend to say *thanks for your interest* to all of them. This becomes pretty time consuming so I quickly decide to update my profile with a note that I don't respond to flirts (one click sends a flirt) and that real messages get my attention.

I noticed one gentleman had sent a couple real messages of interest. He was very complimentary so I gathered he actually read my whole profile and the conversation began. Nice guy, college professor, successful, polite family man and *very* good looking, I might add. We had a lot in common except the spiritual thing; discovered this after a few conversations. Now my profile clearly stated that my preference is someone who actively shares my faith. *Well,* many talk the talk but aren't really walking it. And it turned out, that the photo he posted online was at least 20 years old. I later learned that's called "catfishing" - where the pics don't reflect one's current appearance. Ok, next!

Believe it or not, this journey became quite entertaining – like reality TV. Honestly, I have met some very interesting characters, whom I probably would never have met here in my area. Men from all walks of life; some were local, some not and all ages expressed interest – from late 30's (how flattering!) to late 70's. Of course, my preference is in neither of those decades. Quite a few owned their own businesses and were very successful. I encountered gentlemen with varying levels of intelligence and common sense. Widowed, divorced, never married; most were genuine people searching for a meaningful relationship, or just to meet friends.

Of course, there were scammers too; people out to take advantage of lonely women and get money out of them. Yes, it's true. Thank God for discernment! Too many women can't see past their desire for a man in their life and they get sucked in. It takes a keen ear and attention to inconsistencies.

So, I've been on more than one dating site over the years and several times just shut it all down totally (like now). Even though I enjoy meeting new people, it's good to take breaks to reassess and just breathe. My view has been that while I'd love a long-term relationship (maybe remarriage). **I AM WHOLE** whether or not it happens. I have a great life – a blessed life!

I know you're curious for details. The eligible bachelor list below contains fictitious names to "protect the innocent."

- o Joe from Jamaica proposed marriage without ever meeting in person.
- o Peter in Dallas, who owned an online shopping business, was eager to help me start an event planning business. I just needed to relocate, marry him and

invest a couple thousand bucks to grow his business first. Not. Gonna. Happen.

BTW, this 'gentleman' cursed me when I strongly suggested that he not contact me anymore. It was a short phone call.

- ○ George in Cali, extremely intelligent (a turn-on for me), also proposed marriage. We'd have a bi-coastal relationship. I don't think so!
- ○ Henry, a widower originally from the Netherlands, had a young child who needed a mother. The story about his deceased wife changed a couple times. He bought & sold minerals (huh?) and upon arriving in Africa to trade gems, asked me to accept a shipment of electronic equipment to later send to him. Wouldn't cost me anything. Thanks, but no thanks!
- ○ Paul in Atlanta expected me to help raise his then four-year-old brat - I mean son (with discipline issues). Um, I'll pass, thanks.
- ○ Winston was smitten from the very beginning. He was a doting father; a visionary, and a former chef/restaurateur. We actually lived in the same neighborhood in DC years ago, and he jokingly claimed that I rebuffed his advances back then. He loved the Lord and was active in his church. We planned to worship together until the ex-girlfriend reappeared. I warned him but he went back to Egypt.* I think she

was a "friend with benefits" that I didn't offer. Very disappointing.

*Note: *In the Old Testament, God delivered his people (the Israelites) out of slavery imposed by Pharaoh. While on their journey to the land God promised them, they complained constantly and told Moses they'd rather go back to Egypt. They weren't happy with what God provided. That generation never entered the promised land.*

o Tony absolutely loved my profile, especially that God is first in my life. Neither of us had experienced such a dynamic connection spiritually. We had lots in common. Both of us adore our children and grandchildren; love music, movies, food and *lots* of laughter; both serious about our faith. He professed love after dating a couple months and we were super excited about our friendship. Shortly thereafter, totally out of the blue, he announced he wasn't ready for a relationship because it takes work to make it work. I totally respect where others are (and are not) in their journey. But, really?!

Note: Believe me, I didn't hesitate to kindly let this Brother know (he is my brother in Christ) how he influenced my life and that while I appreciated his honesty, I wasn't too happy with his decision, to put it mildly. Not long after the breakup, God miraculously took away the hurt and disappointment I was feeling. **It just lifted!** The lesson: God knows everyone and everything I deal with… the loves, joys, hurts, disappointments, and questions. I truly don't lean on my own understanding. Many times, I **don't** understand. Like what happened with this guy. I trust God who knows all things. His will is perfect. That's enough for me.

That's a lot of people, you say. Yes, I've been on the dating scene for longer than I want to admit. I make friends easily and love the art of conversation. I could chat whenever I wanted to, from the comfort of my home. No makeup, in my comfy PJs – appearance doesn't matter. Conversation ranged from deep theological doctrine to family matters, to life experiences, and many times downright silliness. That I loved. In all fairness, most were decent, respectable, sincere and hard-working men. I only met a few in person. Most were restricted to email and/or phone conversations only. Some just wanted friendly conversation.

In this stage of life, men and women both desire a great relationship but many carry the heavy baggage of past hurts. So, they're really not ready for someone new. Unforgiveness, bitterness, trust issues, preconceived notions of the opposite sex, self-centeredness and worldly views about the roles of men and women taint one's perspective. I've been told by several men that finding a good woman is like searching for a needle in a haystack and they considered me wifey material. However, when some find one; hmm, turns out they're not really ready themselves, although they think they are.

Interestingly, a friend that I met online shortly before my oldest daughter married, encouraged me to write – to memorialize my feelings around that time. Hence, the poem contained in this book entitled *Prelude To Forever*.

I sincerely hope that everyone searching for that special someone finds him/her. And life goes on.

How's your love life? We are to respect others – no matter the nature of the connection. Could be a bestie, a family member, a coworker, or that special someone. Find it hard to love some people who might not look like you, think like you, love like you? Go to 1 Corinthians 13 in the New Testament for a reminder of what love looks like.

CHAPTER EIGHTEEN

Words With Friends

Yes, I play games on Facebook. Realizing that it can become addictive and a huge time-waster, it does have its merit according to proven research! Some games can help relax the mind; some are great brain stimulators. I find playing games a much better option than watching TV. (That's another story!)

This online word game is like the good ole' Scrabble word game and fun. I have played four or more games simultaneously with family and friends. I fare pretty well, being an excellent speller, and manage to squash a few. I admit that I've been absolutely squashed by some as well. You choose who you want to challenge and you can also play total strangers; those who are not your "friends." No harm there. Of course, I never extend a friend invite to anyone I don't know.

True friendship is a gift. How does that happen? Sometimes it's immediate when first meeting someone. You feel like soulmates; a sister or brother from another mother. Or you *are* related by blood. You just click. You're kindred spirits. You think alike. You like the same things. You view the world through the same lens. You feel like twins.

Some friendships develop over a period of time. You have years of shared experiences. You grew up together, attended school together or lived in the same neighborhood. Whatever the circumstances, friends become special people in our lives with whom we can laugh and cry. They stay close during the most difficult times and they share in times of celebration and great joy. Some may be close for a season then drift away. When they return, it's like there was no separation. You just pick up where you left off.

I believe people come into our lives for specific reasons. Some stay for a short time, others for a lifetime. For some, we may never know their real purpose. I bet you can think of a few in your life that fit in that category. Some teach us valuable lessons. Some learn from us. Some are there to encourage and uplift us while others are true thorns in the flesh. We can learn from them all… patience, longsuffering, kindness, forgiveness, empathy, and unselfishness. We can learn when to speak and when to be silent.

It's important to realize that our words are powerful. Did you know that what you say can bring things into existence? Example, if I tell myself over and over that I will never accomplish anything. Guess what? I'll never accomplish anything. If I tell myself that I can't do whatever, I'll never do it. It seems to me that there are forces out there that don't want me to think positively about anything and if I give in to that, my world will be pretty grim. If I give into the "voices" right now, at this very moment telling me that no one will like this book; I'll not finish or share it. You know which path I took.

The point is this: There is power in what we say. There are old biblical proverbs that talk about the words we use. They tell us that the tongue has the power of life and death, that smart folks use words with restraint, that soothing words are the tree of life and that words can also crush one's spirit. Also, harsh words stir up anger while gentle words have the opposite effect; gossip goes deep and there is joy in giving proper and timely advice. You can get the full verbiage in the book of Proverbs in the Old Testament of the Bible, chapters 15, 17, and 18.

I smile when I think of the friends I've made over the years. Every one of you are treasured gifts! And I'm grateful to walk my journey with you. You color my world. Some I've worked with. Some I've worshipped with regularly. Some share my love of jazz. Some just tolerate me (and that's okay). Some I've had to let go, and some I've only known for a short period. There are those who called themselves "friends," but the opposite proved true. Then there are the few really special people whom I've adopted into my family. Sisters and brothers from another mother. Everyone is not meant to be in that category and you know who you are. You are willing vessels of God's love to me and others. You may not even know the depth of the impact you've had in my life and it continues.

When around friends, no matter the nature of the connection, what are our words? Are they words that build up or tear down? Do we show respect and appreciation or do we engage in negative talk? Does the conversation profit anyone or do we have a spirit of discontent, complaining about everything? Do we project a victim attitude – woe is me? I find that it's easy to go down that road especially when circumstances are not the most desirable.

Novel thought: We can find something good just about everywhere. Blessings in disguise. At times, it may take a minute to see those blessings. We have to look for them, be of the mindset that nothing really happens by chance or luck. Have the attitude that something good is about to happen and when things don't go as planned, we can learn from them. That's a blessing – to realize that everything has a purpose, even when we may not understand it totally or at all. This is true for us all and quite comforting to hear such words from our friends, our allies. Words that lift us up, that give hope in the bleakest moments.

I've been there and I'm sure the same is true for you. In a time or place where it seems there is no hope. At those times, encouraging support from loved ones make a world of difference. It doesn't change anything, but it helps in dealing with it. My closest circle of family and friends – and it's a small circle – choose words and actions that restore my faith and give comfort during hard times. The question should not be "Why me?" (which we all tend to do), but "Why *not* me?"

This may sound crazy, but one of the benefits of struggle is being able to empathize and support others when they face similar challenges. Because, it's not just about you or me but how we can serve others with compassion and genuine care.

So, let's guard our words with friends and strangers and realize the impact we have. Often, we may also need to be our own best friend and encourage ourselves in our journeys. If we practice speaking positively to and about ourselves, it will be easier to do the same for others.

Encouragement and appreciation leave us feeling valued. It's absolutely true that people may not remember what you say or do. They will surely remember how you made them feel.

CHAPTER NINETEEN

"What I Say?"

𝕳ave you ever been in a conversation and the person you're talking with not hear one word you've said? Have you been that person? My dear Mama would say something to us kids (usually instruction about our behavior) and then ask us to repeat what she said. "Now, what I say?" She also said "If you can't hear, you can feel." In other words, she did not spare the rod in disciplining her four children. Many times, we had to line up oldest to youngest for our "discipline" – aka spankings – that took place in the little pantry just off the kitchen. Being the youngest, I had to wait my turn to get mine, after my hoodlum - I mean deeply loved - siblings.

First, let's clarify one thing – I didn't do anything wrong! And I'd have my chance to declare my innocence soon... after standing outside the pantry door and hearing my siblings proclaim the same. Mama had us trained pretty well. Yelling and screaming while being disciplined was not allowed. We had to stand still and take our punishment. Besides, the pantry was really too small to even try to get away. Smart woman, my mother! First, she'd send us outdoors to pick our own switches which were tiny branches off bushes in the yard. Hmm, plenty of bushes were on our property. Was that the real reason for the beautiful landscaping? LOL! These switches left no marks on the skin... and my mother would sternly repeat, "This hurts me more than it hurts you." Yeah, right! That was my thought as a child. I totally understood what she was saying and feeling when I had to discipline my own children decades later. That's another story in itself.

"Mama, I didn't do anything! It was Donnie & Gary," I proclaimed as I whimpered with each stinging blow. Her answer, "I'm sure I missed something!" Of course, I thought she was cruel and mean. That's another story too.

Fast forward. As we grew, she would have us repeat what she said and it could be a conversation about anything. She could sense when we were not fully listening, distracted by other things; not really hearing her. Most times we did hear but not really listening as she suspected.

"Where are you going with this, Joan," you ask. How often do we not really hear what God is saying to us in His Word? We're not really listening. How often do we not really believe what Scripture says?... about anything? How often are we distracted by the cares of this world, not paying attention and hearing God speaking to us? Do we really believe He is forgiving, caring and in tune with our lives today? Do we want to listen? I'm guilty of being preoccupied with the cares of my heart, the cares of this world and not listening. I will tell you that hearing God has to be intentional. You will not hear him "speak to you" unless you first want to hear His voice and then stay plugged in long enough to hear it. Your ears must be open to hear him. This must be a daily process for me. I want to hear God. I want His guidance and wisdom 'cause I've surely made lots of mistakes in my lifetime.

Here's a glimpse of how this is true for me. Anticipating turning 30 *again*, I decided to throw a big bash to celebrate. I made a list of exactly what I wanted this party to be: the guest list, the place, the color scheme, catering, the cake, the location, the weather, etc. And I prayed fervently about every detail. The place was a big consideration. Being a beach lover, I thought it would be fabulous to celebrate there. I decided against that option after considering distance, expense, etc., for my guests. Near the end of this planning process, just before the party, I felt God saying that He graciously granted my wishes for this thing. I trusted and fervently prayed for this one event and trusted that He would answer my prayers. How about areas of my life that really matter! How about seeking Him fervently for issues that I think I can handle or actually ignore? Thinking that it'll all work out, believing that all things work for my good. I felt Him saying that isn't enough. I should have deep conversation with Him about every area of my life.

I'm here to tell you that He is who He says He is. I'm now realizing and seeing ever so clearly HIS presence in every area and I take everything to Him; happy, sad and indifferent. He knows every longing of my heart. Every. Little. Thing. He cares about every little thing. Don't believe the lie in your mind that it can't be true, even if a thousand hardships and disappointments come to mind. Don't be like Eve in the Garden, when the serpent asked her if God really said what He said.

These last few years have been an amazing run... not saying there's not been trials and hardships. Hey! Some of you know my trials. You've been in the trenches with me. That's part of the journey. That's when I "feel" His presence the most; when things don't go as I hoped. The thing is that God cares about you too. Taste and see the goodness of the Lord! You have nothing to lose. Get to know Him for yourself.

So, I imagine God saying the same thing Mama used to say.

Do you have a personal relationship with God? It's free! No prep needed. Just go to Him wherever you are in your journey.

CHAPTER TWENTY

Renew Your Mind

I find myself talking about this quite a lot; the importance of reducing negativity. It surrounds us. It's steeped in our culture. Seemingly, tearing people down is a form of entertainment to many. Does it really profit anyone? Does it make anyone feel better?

On a personal note (and it is personal), we must not only control what enters our space but we must be aware of what we say to ourselves. It seems to come so naturally; to tear oneself down. I think we don't even notice it. It's become a habit because we hear it from others, from social media, the Internet, TV, and sometimes our parents. Yes, our culture has bred generations of negative talk, and well-meaning parents fall into negativity without even thinking about it most times because that's all they know. I'm guilty too. That's a discussion for another time.

Right now, let's talk about how we can fill our minds with positive talk about ourselves; renewing our frame of mind. I've been reading a lot more in the past 2-3 years about personal development. We can never stop learning to be our best selves.

Monitoring and changing my thought patterns are part of developing myself to be my best self.

A widely popular exercise is to practice words of affirmation. Similar to recognizing our best qualities, affirmation is about validating our best selves, no matter what we might think. No matter what others may say or think of us, it is confirming the positive. So, what if I don't think I'm all that? What if I'm so mired in negative self-talk that I don't realize what I'm really saying to me about myself? That's just it. How often, if ever, do we stop and think about what we say? Not often... Not often enough. We just poke along accepting whatever thoughts pop into our minds.

Renewing one's mind has to be intentional. We have to pay attention to what comes out of our mouths... What thoughts do we plant into our subconscious mind? We should listen to ourselves and take stock of whether we speak positively or negatively.

Here are a few examples of negative talk:

- I can't do that.
- I'm no good at that.
- Oh, stupid me!
- I'm too shy.
- I never know what to say.
- I never get a break.
- I'll never get it right.
- I'm just not cut out for that.

- I can't handle this.
- That's impossible.
- Everything I touch turns to ____.
- I never win anything.
- It's not in the cards for me.
- Nobody likes me.
- Seems like I'm always broke.
- If only I was taller.
- If only I was skinnier.
- I'm not good with names.
- It's no use.
- Things never go right for me.

You get the idea. I've made many of these statements myself. The more we say and think this way, the more we believe it. I'm working on cutting it out! It's a work in progress. How to change that? Sounds like a lot of work. We must learn to take **every** thought captive. Examine it and eliminate the bad stuff. What we say becomes our belief and what we believe governs our actions.

I remember being teased at work because I talked to myself (and answered). Admittedly, it probably wasn't positive most of the time! You know, fussing at the computer or the software or office equipment because it wasn't cooperating. We laughed. Ok, I laughed at myself and owned up to it. The standard reply was something like "I'm my best audience" and "No one else listens to me like me!" I digress a bit.

What I've learned to do, in this vein of renewing my mind, is to make a list of positive affirmations to say aloud every day. Most days I do. They're in plain sight on a vision board in my bedroom.

Here are a few of my affirmations. The more I say them, the deeper is my belief:

- I am God's masterpiece, fearfully & wonderfully made.
- I am never alone.
- I am fulfilled.
- I am blessed.
- Good things are coming my way.
- Good things are happening for me.
- Good things are manifesting for me.
- Good things are attracted to me.
- I am worthy of my dreams.
- I am teachable.
- I am loving.
- I am highly favored.
- I am gifted.
- I am free.
- I am a winner.
- I am appreciated.
- I am chosen.
- I am called.
- I am successful.
- I am grateful.

- o   I am loved.
- o   I am valued and respected.
- o   I am enough.

Seeing and saying these affirmations regularly boosts my faith. It keeps me in the proper frame of mind, especially when challenges arise and when I'm tempted to doubt myself and others. The truth is that I am unique and so are you!

Other important habits to develop in this process include (1) surrounding oneself with positive people. That means we just may need to get rid of some friends and be open to embrace new ones; (2) monitoring what we take in via TV, social media, magazines, movies, etc. I love movies and like to be entertained. Comedies, a little suspense and drama are fine. I don't find gratuitous violence or horror entertaining at all. I also find sexually explicit movies and music rather degrading. You have to make your own judgments. I am selective about what I consume and so should you be.

Speaking of judgments, I find that having a sympathetic and compassionate ear towards others is also helpful. You might ask," How does that relate to renewing your mind?" It is another element of keeping a positive outlook, in general. Often, we make snap judgments about others without really knowing their story and the opinions we form are usually not good or correct. I say give everyone the benefit of the doubt. We don't really know others' challenges and circumstances until we walk in their shoes. Affirming who you are on a regular basis will affect how you see others as well. Think you can't do it? Change that statement to the positive. Yes, you can!

Reversing a lifelong habit takes time and it may seem challenging when you really are not feeling it. You're not feeling like a winner or a conqueror because of circumstances. Believe me, I can relate. I've been there. A specific day comes to mind and my life seemed to be crashing down around me. I stood in my bedroom, crying and shouting my affirmations. I needed to do that at that moment. I wasn't feeling successful, or valued or appreciated. Felt crushed by things happening around me and to me; things outside of my control. It was a healing moment and I didn't realize it at the time. Doing so enabled me to navigate through very difficult times. It is real.

Interestingly, this exercise – writing this book – really builds up my faith that ordinary people like me really can positively affect the lives of others. I push away doubtful thoughts that occur as I write… because I truly believe every one of us is gifted. Sharing our gifts and talents not only brings blessings to us, but also to everyone in our circles of influence. How cool is that?! I am deeply grateful to find my voice.

 I encourage you to never give up.
You are worth it.
You are valuable.
You are important.
This world would not be the same without you.
You have purpose.

CHAPTER TWENTY-ONE

Ramblings

"Sometimes 1 sits and thinks, and sometimes I just sit." Somewhere in time, I heard someone say that. It could've been one of the Three Stooges. I don't know.

Today, remembering a fun gathering over the weekend past. I look at the group picture of us posing & waving. We had such a blast. The gathering was hosted by one of my favorite cousins. She's actually an in-law but you'd never think so. We clicked when we met, during the time she first met her hubby's extended family. She's not from these parts. The then-newlyweds met at college down South. She says that she's an introvert. NOT! We laugh about that. She is super talented and lives her life in full color. She actively shares her musical gift, has released several CD's in the last five years and is such an inspiration to me and many others. Just do it! She's a joy to be around and she loves spoiling her sister-friends. This group of ladies - we are her number one fans. These ladies are now part of my circle too. We don't see each other often, but when we do, there's always lots of laughs and pure fun.

So, my point is this: It's important to surround oneself with positive people who bring smiles to your heart. And it turns into a mutual thang! I am grateful for each of them.

Just a thought: JUDGE JOAN – Not! It's so very easy to judge others. Many times, we make judgments based on preconceived perceptions. We make judgments when we think we really know people. This is not good. It seems that we women do this to a fault. We make assumptions and form opinions based on appearance, or what we hear (gossip) or what we think we saw. We're so ready to tear others down rather than build them up. Wouldn't it be great if we accepted people without judgment wherever they are in their journey? Realize that we have more in common than not. Wouldn't it be great if we celebrated each other, supported, respected and appreciated each other – no matter what season of life? That would certainly foster a stronger sense of community among us.

Everyone has a story. Everyone's journey is unique. Until we walk in another's shoes, we can't fully understand why they do what they do; or why they think the way they think. Rather than draw conclusions, how about a little conversation! That's the key to understanding. Too often we're afraid to engage because it might not be a comfortable exchange. Well, *geesh* – it might be an enjoyable and friendly exchange. If we listen more than talk, progress can be made. Both parties would benefit and come away with a better understanding of the other.

This came to mind as I reviewed my writings. The last thing I want to communicate to readers is that my views on faith or spiritual matters makes me better than anyone else. It does not. I do not want to convey that my faith makes me "holier than thou." We are alike in many ways yet different in many ways – in how we view the world. Our vantage point may be positively or negatively influenced by life experiences, our upbringing, early and current environment, circumstances out of our control, and those in our lives who have had great influence (parents, teachers, neighbors, etc.). We maneuver life differently and at different paces and spaces in time. The important thing to remember is that we all will "graduate" at some point in time. We all will "pass on" at our appointed time… A former coworker used to say "None of us gets outta here alive." Let's enjoy the ride together!...

Just a thought.

Can I say something else? Don't you think I have a unique writing style? I call it descriptive writing. It sometimes takes a minute to get to the point. It's like a drive in the country. You know where you're going, but there's a yard sale on the side of the road and I'm sure there's something at that sale I need because everything's only $1.00. It takes time to browse and then you get back on the road. Hopefully I don't get hungry on the way, that means a munch break; another diversion. BUT it makes the trip memorable, right? Of course, it does!

OR, as my Mother would say: "Going around Robin Hood's barn." I got the gist of what she was saying... but Robin Hood's barn? Never knew he had a barn! I should've asked Mama about that. It was one of many old sayings. That's another story too.

Maybe I should've put this at the beginning of the book to prepare you!

Do you ever ramble in words or thought? Sometimes it's good to vent to process information mentally. Don't forget to discard the negatives, draw out the positives; then move on.

CHAPTER TWENTY-TWO

Surrender

My spiritual journey is ever evolving. I rejoice in that because, for many years, I seemed to be on autopilot. I must confess that while I prayed and worshipped regularly, it's just been recently that I find myself really wanting more; to actually know God better. How did I get here? Crisis. It's very humbling to admit it out loud.

Crisis. Yup, that's the truth. You might ask why I choose to share this detail. It's because I know I'm not alone. I suspect that many of you may be at the same place.

As much as I like to tell myself that "I got this," God has opened my eyes to see how far from the truth that statement really is. I surrender my "Independent, Strong Black Woman" card to obtain His truth and will for me. This can be a painful process for some of us; for those whose life has required them to be in control; take charge. We develop expectations. We face trials and challenges and we are pushed to "get it done." It makes us resilient and tough and hardens us, even as women. The result is that we find it difficult to truly rely on God. We say we do but we actually become our own savior. We don't need

God. Oh, we may call on Him from time to time for some things – the things we know that we really can't or don't want to control; like waving a magic wand. How about the small things and the deep longings of our hearts? Do we trust Him in those areas?

Not long ago, God started a conversation and this is what He said:

> JOAN, Do you really believe I am who I say I am? You say you do. You come to me about this and about that... like money needed for bills, like a particular event, like issues that you face. That's great! You've seen my faithfulness over the years. Well, how about that secret area of your heart? Do you trust me behind closed doors? You will never see my full power in your life until you release those secret things that you don't tell anyone about.

This was a vivid conversation in my mind and the journey began. He brings different areas to mind that I need to submit to him, that I CAN take to Him. And He helps me do just that. My belief (faith) has skyrocketed, just as I consider His faithfulness, His answers to my prayers... I have joy at a level I've never experienced before. It makes me want to take everything to Him! It's awesome to me that He helps me and desires that I "walk this way."

Recently, while attending a corporate training event, I learned the following insights. (Psst, we have to be teachable, no matter what age.) To get a breakthrough in any area of our lives, there is a process.

#1 – We are faced with a crisis. It causes us to stop in our tracks. It could be financial, personal, work-related, etc.

#2 – Turn to God. We should seek God for help; emphasis on *should*. This requires us to walk in faith; believing that He hears, answers, and guides.

#3 – Move on Up. Following God's guidance/instruction (must wait on Him and obey), we experience a higher level of faith; deeper knowledge.

#4 – Repeat. Get ready to learn something new, face a new challenge to grow even more.

Notice any similarity to how I talked about surrendering? Any similarity to your journey? Romans 5:3-5 talks about how we *"glory in our sufferings"* because it produces perseverance and that produces character and so on and so on. Psalm 25:5 is my earnest prayer: *"Guide me in Your truth and teach me, for You are God my Savior, and my hope is in you all day long."*

Are there areas in your life where you need a breakthrough? Be encouraged. It's worth the effort to gain knowledge, grow deeper and go higher. You'll find yourself in a better place, with deeper faith, a sense of accomplishment and resolve to tackle challenges head-on.

CHAPTER TWENTY-THREE

Poetic Expressions

MUSINGS
Early morning
Just waking
Foggy
Thinking
Still

Pondering
Questioning
Reflecting
Tearful
Irritated

They said this
They said that
I believed
Gullible
Too trusting
Emotional

Unsure
Fickle
Frustrated
Tired
Alone is good
For now

Funny but not
Coffee
Tears
Release
Drowsy

Hungry
Who listens
Who cares
Need a hug
Thinking

Quiet
Good
Resting
Throw a pillow
Wanna scream

Breathe deeply
Again
Again
I needed that

THE EXCHANGE

Holidays!
Pull away from the strum of daily beats
Exchange one rhythm for another

Bask in family warmth
Ponder the year past and the new year upon us
Many with aching hearts

Cherish times with loved ones no longer within reach
Exchange sorrow for joy
Celebrate connections that are soft mists in our memories

Christmas, a new welcoming
A remembrance of the great exchange
Between Glory and humanity
Indeed, the greatest gift
Far exceeding temporal gifts

Renewed hope for the new year
Exchanging discontentment for contentment
Hard hearts for forgiveness and compassion
Bitterness for gratitude
Self-centeredness for empathy

Remember the Greatest Exchange
Show love to the seemingly unlovable
Count your blessings, One by one.

PRELUDE TO FOREVER
For My Daughter's Wedding in 2010

The guests are seated, awaiting the processional - willing
partners and witnesses.
Anticipation rises as the music of two lives becoming one
serenade them.

He stands facing them,
Assuring each silently of his intentions to cover her with
his cloak of husbandry.
He awaits her entrance.

Soft petals pave the way for her delicate feet.
She appears, her glow illuminating the path to her
beloved.

Radiant, she slowly, gracefully and deliberately strolls
toward him.
Their hearts leap and race to greet the other...

Heavenly breezes usher in the spirit of the Lord
As he joins their souls in holy matrimony.
It is a beginning; it is an end to life once known...

Celebration and rejoicing deliver their vows unto the
realms of glory...
A new day has begun; the old has passed away.

It is the Prelude to Forever...

THE ELUSIVE ONE

Waking to the soothing ocean breezes
He stands above me
Face shielded by the bright sun

His voice is calming
As the ebb and flow of the tide
Steady, sure, tender
Refreshing.

He reaches for me
And I for him
But we can't seem to connect
My outstretched arms feel his warmth
But not his touch

Extending further
Can't seem to reach far enough
To fully grasp
And he fades away
To the recesses of my mind.

The glow of his smile lingers
And his fragrance fills the air
Enveloping and
Tickling my senses

Repositioning
Reinventing
Realizing the dream of fulfillment desired

Breathlessly stirring
Awaiting his return
To behold his grace
Imagining his soul embracing mine... And I exhale.

Is there a Poet or Writer hiding in you? What is your passion? Romans 12 says that each of us is gifted and our gifts can be used to serve, teach and encourage others, and more. If you died today... what dreams, what ideas, what talents, what giftedness would die with you? Your world is waiting!

CHAPTER TWENTY-FOUR

Follow Your Road

I heard a song with that title "back in the day" while visiting my sister in Philadelphia. I remember it clearly. On a beautiful Sunday afternoon, we joined some of her friends for a cookout in the park. This tune, recorded by a Christian jazz band, began to play. I had not heard it or of them before that day, and became an instant fan. I found the lyrics captivating and thought-provoking. It spoke about how sometimes we don't know where our lives may lead – which road to take, because there are many. We may wonder where a particular road will lead, but we won't know if we don't go. They sang of how we are travelers in a foreign land (this life) trying to find our way, looking for answers. The main point was that we should not be afraid to move forward and that we have to follow our road. That point was repeated several times.

As a relatively new Christian and a single mother at that time, I wondered where my road would lead. Listening to that song made me think. In any season of life, we surely wonder what the future holds. Maybe we're not where we thought we'd be by a certain age. Maybe we've grown comfortable where we are; complacent with how things are. Maybe circumstances forced us to postpone our dreams. Or maybe we rely on the approval of others and allow their opinions to sway us. Or could it be that past failures have paralyzed us and we're afraid to try again?

Fear = **F**alse **E**vidence **A**ppearing **R**eal. We fear failure. But failure is a necessary step to success. We have to give ourselves permission to fail and learn from it. How many times does a baby fall when learning to walk? If the car doesn't start, don't we try again? There's a poem that says "If at first you don't succeed, try, try again." I learned it in elementary school. But we seem to forget that as we get older. We depend too much on what others think. We seek approval from people who may not really know us or care about us.

I have to share another story ripped from the pages of my life. I will never ever forget it. I was at the beach (my favorite place!) with my sister and two Sista-Girl-Cousins. We had just celebrated the son's wedding of one of these cousins. We decided to relax at the beach for a few days afterward. We were enjoying perfect beach weather this early September day.

Basking in the sun, each of us went for a solitary stroll along the water's edge. After my walk, I sat with the new Mother-in-law—Sista-Girl-cousin. Plugged into her music with the serenity of the calming waves, she took her earplugs out, turned to me, looked me straight in the face and said this. "The Lord wants you to know that you do not need to be validated by any man. You do not need to be validated by your job.... and you do not need to be validated by your church. I have given you *everything you need* to do what I have called you to do!" The tears streamed down my face as she spoke. I get misty every time I think about it... like right now as I share this with you. I was speechless! My cousin then said that she didn't know where that came from. *I knew.* She said that she had not planned to say anything like that to me. It just came out. Then she asked me to repeat it because she could not remember exactly what she said. Well, I was done. I just sat there and cried, with the ocean roaring in the background.

You see, I knew my gifts but I wanted approval and was *afraid* to fully explore them. I apparently cared too much about what others thought of me. There's nothing wrong with wanting to be liked... but it had somewhat stifled me and I got comfortable in my pretty, little, self-constructed, velvet-lined jewelry box. Gifts (my talents) that are bestowed upon me are not meant for me to keep to myself but are meant to be given away. These gifts create within me a rich opportunity to become more than a receiver. If I only focus on the getting of gifts, then I miss out on the blessing of becoming a giver. The gift increases the more I share it with others and loses its value if it only remains with me. The same is true for you.

Take a look at *your* life, *your* journey... Get up and go where your heart leads you. Otherwise, your gifts and talents just get dusty, hidden behind the locked doors of your heart. You know what will be the result? Regret for not stepping out and making it happen. Who wants regrets at the end of life? - for not fully LIVING?

Are you where you planned to be at this point in your life journey? Have disappointments made you afraid to follow your dreams because failure may raise its ugly head... again? I encourage you to push forward!

"Always remember that your present situation is not your final destination. The best is yet to come."
Zig Ziglar

JEWELS INDEX

TOPICAL INDEX by chapter

RESOURCES

Scriptures Referenced - New International Version (NIV)

Chapter Six: Believe You Me

- 1 John 4:19 *"We love because he first loved us."*
- Hebrews 13:5 *"... because God has said, 'Never will I leave you; never will I forsake you.'"*
- Jeremiah 29:11-13 *"For I know the plans I have for you,"* declares the Lord, *"plans to prosper you and not to harm you, plans to give you hope and a future. Then you will call on me and come and pray to me, and I will listen to you. You will seek me and find me when you seek me with all your heart..."*

Chapter Seven: Be Still

- 1 Corinthians 13:4-8, 13 *"Love is patient, love is kind. It does not envy, it does not boast, it is not proud. It does not dishonor others, it is not self-seeking, it is not easily angered, it keeps no record of wrongs. Love does not delight in evil but rejoices with the truth. It always protects, always trusts, always hopes, always perseveres. Love never fails... And now these three remain: faith, hope and love. But the greatest of these is love."*

Chapter Eighteen: Words With Friends

- Proverbs 15, 17, and 18 (Excerpts)
  - Chapter 15:1, 4, 23 *"A gentle answer turns away wrath, but a harsh word stirs up anger.... The soothing tongue is a tree of life, but a perverse tongue crushes the spirit.... A person finds joy in giving an apt reply—and how good is a timely word!"*
  - Chapter 17: 27 *"The one who has knowledge uses words with restraint..."*
  - Chapter 18: 8, 21 *"The words of a gossip are like choice morsels; they go down to the inmost parts.... The tongue has the power of life and death, and those who love it will eat its fruit."*

Chapter Twenty-Two: Surrender

- Romans 5:3-5 *"Not only so, but we also glory in our sufferings, because we know that suffering produces perseverance; perseverance, character; and character, hope. And hope does not put us to shame, because God's love has been poured out into our hearts through the Holy Spirit, who has been given to us."*
- Psalm 25:5 *"Guide me in Your truth and teach me, for you are God my Savior, and my hope is in you all day long."*

Chapter Twenty-Three: Poetic Expressions

- Romans 12:6-8 *"We have different gifts, according to the grace given to each of us. If your gift is prophesying, then prophesy in accordance with your faith; if it is serving, then serve; if it is teaching, then teach; if it is to encourage, then give encouragement; if it is giving, then give generously; if it is to lead, do it diligently; if it is to show mercy, do it cheerfully."*

ABOUT THE AUTHOR

Joan Curtis Waters

Joan retired from the world of human resources and firmly believes that the greatest resource for all humans is the Lord God Almighty. She also has 18+ years of experience coordinating corporate and private events, hosts annual tea parties for ladies of all ages and from all walks of life, and has enthusiastically volunteered to serve her community in various roles over the years. She brings passion to everything her hands touch and sees humor in everyday life.

Joan is the proud mother of two amazingly gifted daughters Rashida and Jill; Gigi to three exceptionally bright grandchildren DeKare, Maya and Devin; and mother-in-law to the greatest son-in-law ever, Demetri.

A people-lover, Joan seeks to inspire, encourage and celebrate others. Her claim to fame is being a family-aholic, and a self-proclaimed expert on Chesapeake Bay crab cakes and Southern Maryland stuffed ham. Joan treasures time with family and friends, JAZZ, laughing out loud, endless days at the beach, world travel and life in general.

Made in the USA
Lexington, KY
04 December 2019